Get SMART!

Five Steps Toward a Healthy Brain

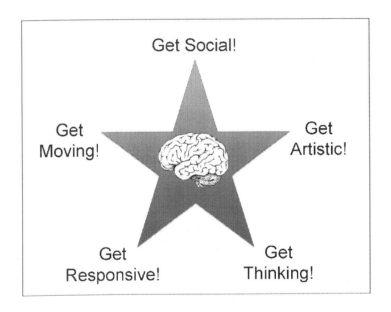

Get Social!

Get
Moving!

Get
Artistic!

Get
Responsive!

Get
Thinking!

Arthur Shimamura, Ph.D.

This book is dedicated to family, friends, colleagues, and students who have shared with me so many fun and exciting adventures. May you all enjoy healthy brains and lifelong learning.

CONTENTS

Preface   i

Chapter 1: Get Started!   1

Chapter 2: Get Social!   20

Chapter 3: Get Moving!   36

Chapter 4: Get Artistic!   56

Chapter 5: Get Responsive!   74

Chapter 6: Get Thinking!   93

Epilogue   116

References and Resources   121

Preface

When my two sons were young, they'd spend their summer vacations sitting in front of the TV playing video games and looking as bored in their virtual reality as in real life. As a university professor, my summers included time off from teaching with a more intense focus on my research projects on human memory and learning. In an attempt to instill an inkling of intellectual fervor in my boys, or at least some form of brain activity, I began thinking about daily activities for them that could facilitate mental engagement and fitness.

I initiated an "active learning" summer program. My boys would have to demonstrate weekly accomplishments in four domains: reading, writing, art, and exercise. As an incentive, I gave each a blank notebook and told them that their writing and art projects could be fulfilled by a one-page write-up of the week's events paired with a drawing. The actual incentive was the promise (bribe) of cash at the end of the summer for completing the program. I didn't realize it at the time, but my reward turned out to be notebooks filled with writings and drawings from summers long ago (as well as two adult sons who are forever stimulating my own brain with their intellectual prowess).

As a well-worn member of the baby boomer generation, I must now contend with my own extended vacation, a time people call *retirement*. I suspect we all try to find ways to stimulate our minds and bodies, though it seems very easy to fall prey to stale routines and cozy habits. I worry that at week's end I'll ask myself, "What have I accomplished?" It's not that we need to justify our existence outside the workplace, and I don't mean to fill you with guilt-ridden sentiments of laziness. My aim is to encourage a broad-based program for brain fitness—a way of fully engaging our brains and ourselves throughout life.

When it comes to promoting healthy aging, we've all heard the phrase, "Use it or lose it!" Yet how we use it is not fully described. Scientists have informed us of how our bodies and brains deteriorate with age, and those aching joints and moments of forgetfulness are frequent reminders. As Bette Davis famously said, "Old age ain't no place for sissies." The good news is that research has also shown that there are ways of caring for ourselves and increasing our chances of aging successfully. What follows is my own "summer vacation" brain fitness program based on what we know about aging and what we can do to foster a healthy brain.

Chapter 1: Get Started!

What do you do in your spare time? In my experience, the most common answer from friends and colleagues is, "What spare time?!" There are certainly periods in one's life—while raising young children or beginning a new career—when it seems difficult to grasp moments of relaxation. There are other times—such as retirement—when spare time is essentially the entire day. Our culture considers it a virtue to be "working" all the time, and we may feel guilty when taking time off. I would contend that we all have spare time. Even the busiest individuals I know spend time (or some might say waste it) doing such things as social networking (*Facebook*, *Twitter*, email), browsing news sites and blogs, watching TV, playing video games, or shopping for things online. I admit guilt to all of these fun activities.

The point is not to demean these spare moments but to develop ways of making leisure time more enriching. Throughout my career, I have been interested in how the brain learns and remembers. Early on I studied individuals with organic amnesia, a brain disorder in which memory for everyday events are virtually absent, though early memories, such as those acquired before brain injury, are generally intact. These individuals know who they are, have normal intelligence, and can converse with ease. Yet due to damage in an area of the brain called the *medial temporal lobe*, they are incapable of storing new experiences encountered since their brain injury (some may have seen the movie, *Memento*, which portrays a character with such a disorder). Medial temporal amnesia is analogous to being able to playback old videos recorded earlier but not able to record any new programs. In the severest of cases, amnesic patients may not remember what had occurred only minutes ago. As Alzheimer's disease begins in the medial temporal lobe, such patients also exhibit this form of memory impairment.

From studies of individuals with brain disorders and also from studies of the normal aging process, we are beginning to understand how different brain regions interact with each other to give us the ability to learn, pay attention, communicate with others, and reminisce about the past. Brain imaging techniques, such as *functional magnetic resonance imaging* (or *fMRI*), have given scientists a window into brain activity as it unfolds in time. I could put you in a MRI scanner— similar to those used in hospitals today—and observe your brain's response as you try to recollect a past event, such as a birthday party or what you had for dinner yesterday.

The application of fMRI to view brain activity would have been considered science fiction only a few decades ago. The technology is now easily implemented and available in many research institutions and universities. Indeed, its use has completely revolutionized psychological science as researchers can now identify brain regions that are active when we respond to sights, sounds, thoughts, and feelings. Recent findings have shown that we can actually use brain activity to determine what you're doing now, such as looking at a beach scene or just mind wandering—almost as if we can read your mind!

I have been fortunate to witness tremendous advances in brain sciences. I have always considered my "work" to be more play than duty, though I always made an effort to set aside time during the day for activities outside my profession. Early on it was primarily evenings with family and time committed to a regular exercise program. In my youth I was on a swim team, and throughout my adult life I have continued my workouts in the pool. I have also tried to indulge my artistic inclinations. When I was in high school I took a photography course and landed a part-time job at a camera store. My parents allowed me to convert a spare bathroom into a darkroom, and I had fun developing black and white prints and expressing myself creatively. That interest waned after college, but twenty years later I took the hobby up again and honed my skills through digital photography workshops during the summer.

So, what *should* you do in your spare time? My answer is: Whatever you want! Yet there is a caveat to that answer as we have learned much about aging and disease and how to reduce their impact on our bodies and brains. If you want to enrich your spare time (and likely have more of it in the future), I offer suggestions based on what scientists have discovered about brain health and mental efficiency. I will not inundate you with graphs, statistical analyses, or detailed methodologies but instead offer general findings and guidelines (references and resources are included at the end of the book).

Who Are You?

Evolutionary biologists will tell you that the only reason for having a brain is for you to pass along your genes to the next generation. For us humans that means having sex (of course) and securing a wealth of resources (food, shelter, high-speed internet). That way, your offspring will have an advantage in transferring their genes. Success in these activities requires the ability to learn from and adapt to environmental changes. Thus our brains have evolved to pick up new information, decide what is good and bad, and remember the consequences of our actions. By this view, we have evolved the ability to learn efficiently and develop a wealth of knowledge so we can garner good sex and sufficient resources.

If that's all there is, as Peggy Lee once sang, then what are we to do with ourselves when we're not reproducing or securing wealth? Presumably, our advanced culture has given us time off from the duties of genetic transfer, and in large part we've co-opted brain function for the purposes of enjoying life. We pass the time socializing with friends, watching TV, surfing the web, going out for entertainment, and just playing around. Evolutionists would argue that even these pastimes point to our need for sex and success. Nevertheless, the bottom line is that we are endowed with the extraordinary capacity to interact with the world and learn from these interactions, and we should use these capabilities whenever we can.

Given our propensity for learning, why aren't we all theoretical physicists or rocket scientists? That kind of expertise requires a specific kind of learning ability—conceptual learning— which we tend to value in our society. Of course, thousands of years ago, such a brainiac would not have been that well suited for the daily goal of killing prey for meals, protecting oneself from predators, and fending off individuals among your own species who would like to make your home and spouse theirs. Back then, having athletic prowess, expertise in weaponry, and good social-communicative skills would likely have been more important for survival. One of our greatest feats of evolution is that we have the extraordinary ability to adapt to changes. Indeed, flexibility may be our strongest asset. In this way, we can become proficient in a multitude of domains. Besides becoming experts at conceptual learning, we can be proficient at sports, music, art, and partying.

Along these lines, the noted psychologist Howard Gardner argued for a pluralistic or multiple view of human intelligence. He identified eight intelligences: linguistic, logic-mathematical, musical, spatial, bodily/kinesthetic, intrapersonal (knowing oneself), interpersonal (knowing ourselves in relation to others), and naturalistic (knowing ourselves in the context of our environment). Gardner drew heavily on brain science as his expertise in brain disorders offered a unique perspective for understanding human intelligence. In fact, his theory of multiple intelligences is based on findings of patients with damage to specific brain areas that cause impairment to particular mental functions, such as verbal, spatial, mathematical, or social ability.

Gardner's theory has influenced educational practices as teaching strategies prior to his work focused on intelligence as a single factor—primarily involving conceptual abilities. This older view does have some credence as individuals who are good at one ability, say mathematics, are often good at others, such as verbal, spatial, or artistic ability. Such findings suggest that there may be a genetic basis for overall brain efficiency, such as neuronal transmission, that would make some people generally good in many domains. On the other hand, some brain regions may be particularly well developed in some individuals. We all can think of that friend or family member who is particularly good (or bad) at one of Gardner's intelligences.

There is ample research to suggest that different brain regions serve different functions. Yet we must also be aware that excellence in any ability, such as being a professional athlete, performing in a major orchestra, obtaining a doctorate, or finding a lifelong mate, requires a multitude of intelligences and the coordination of a network of brain regions. In a nutshell, a healthy mental life depends on activating many brain regions and encouraging a variety of activities. Thus, to address the question, "What is the key to prolonged mental health?" I would answer by paraphrasing an old political aphorism—"It's the whole-brain, stupid!"

The Aging Brain

The human brain consists of a hundred billion neurons, which is comparable to the number of stars in our galaxy. Imagine each neuron connected to a thousand others, and we begin to appreciate the enormous complexity (and potential) of the human brain. Communication between neurons occurs at *synapses*—connection points where chemicals travel between neurons. We begin life with an overabundance of synapses, and through experience these connections are "pruned" such that active synapses strengthen and inactive ones weaken or disappear altogether. Neuroscientists call this process "synaptic plasticity," and a handy saying that captures its essence is *neurons that fire together, wire together*.

Synaptic plasticity is most apparent during early childhood, which enables young children to acquire a language, learn new motor skills, and interact accordingly in social settings (at least most of the time). By age 20 we've lost a third of the synapses we had at infancy. The advantage of synaptic pruning is that we can sculpt our brains in response to our particular environment. This process occurs throughout our lives, though between the ages of 20 and 65 years the overall number of synapses stays fairly constant. After 65, there is a marked decline in available synapses. This diminution in later life hampers communication between neurons and results in those nagging annoyances, such as hearing loss, problems with balance, and forgetfulness. Thankfully, technology in prosthetics, such as hearing aids, walking sticks, and smart phones, have made it easier to deal with those "senior moments" (after a lecture one day, a woman came up to the podium and told me that lately she has experienced so many senior moments that when she remembers something now, she calls it a "junior moment").

The mental challenges we face with aging are many and come from multiple sources. A prime factor is an overall decrease in synaptic efficacy that leads to general slowing of mental processes. Just like a late model automobile, we incur normal wear and tear and just aren't as zippy as we used to be. Indeed, even a well-maintained, ten-year old vehicle won't perform as efficiently as it did when it left the dealership. With use (and abuse) over the years, our brains experience an overall reduction in efficiency. Blood flow may not be as smooth as it used to be, neurons may not fire as efficiently, and synaptic pruning may disrupt neural communication. All of these factors lead to a general slowing of cognitive function as our brains just can't run quite as well on the road as it did when it was new.

In an aging study I conducted a while back, we gave UC Berkeley professors a battery of tests to see if mental abilities in high-functioning individuals (presumably!) differed from typical aging patterns of cognitive decline. Older professors in their 60s and 70s indeed showed well-preserved cognitive abilities and on occasion performed as well as young professors. For example, they were as good as young professors in remembering new conceptual information presented in magazine articles. Such learning proficiency supports the "use it or lose it" notion, as we would expect professors to be proficient at acquiring new information. However on basic tests of reaction time (e.g., responding to the direction indicated by an arrow), these highly functioning professors, showed the same patterns of response slowing as the average adult of similar age. In fact, the number to remember is $1/25^{th}$ of a second, which is the annual decrement in reaction time that we found in participants between the ages of 30 and 71 years. This value doesn't seem very much, but after 30-40 years, such slowing can be the cause of broken hips and mental slips.

When it comes to our thinking brain, we must consider the workings of our two cerebral hemispheres, those large lobes that sit on each side of our head. They are actually two rather broad sheets of neurons. Those folds we see in pictures of the brain are the result of evolution trying to fit an expanding surface into the confines of our rounded skull. When flattened, the size of our cerebral hemispheres is equivalent to an extra large though very thin pizza (about 20 inches in diameter, 2 mm thick). The vast number of neurons that comprise our cerebral cortices are activated in response to the incessant sensations, thoughts, feelings, and movements we experience during every moment of our lives (even during sleep!). If each neuron lit up when it was active, our brains would looks like a pyrotechnic light show. Thus, the myth that we use only 10% of our brain at any given moment is indeed a myth.

With brain imaging techniques, such as fMRI, we have discovered which brain regions light up during specific mental activities, such as seeing, listening, remembering, feeling, and moving. Scientists have applied a useful "subtraction" technique to isolate brain activity related to mental functions. For example, one could have individuals look at a blank screen while at other times keep their eyes closed. By subtracting the "eyes open" brain activity from the "eyes closed" activity, one can isolate brain responses specifically related to vision. By this simple subtraction method, one can start to identify brain circuits associated with just about any particular mental activity. However, in everyday situations, such as carrying on a conversation or reading this book, the entire brain is dynamic and brain regions are working together to processes information. As such, more sophisticated fMRI methods have identified elaborate and overlapping brain circuits that turn on and off depending on the task at hand. With these brain-imaging techniques scientists have had the extraordinary ability to study the human brain in action.

Considering the innumerable situations that our brains confront, it seems incredible that we are able to keep any single thought in mind. Yet, somehow we organize neural activity and control what we are doing (at least most of the time). Try this little demonstration—direct your attention to your breathing and make yourself consciously aware of the air moving in and out of your lungs. Now switch your focus and attend to the pressure on your bottom as you sit. We have the ability to direct and control our mental activity—and you can now stop thinking about your bottom and focus on the next paragraph.

It is your prefrontal cortex, the front 28% of your cerebral hemispheres, that enables you to attend to and control mental activity. Psychologists use the term *executive control* to describe this function. Consider your brain as a large orchestra in which all of the musicians must work together to produce beautiful sound. Without a conductor to control the timing, volume, and rhythm of the players, the music would be disjointed and haphazard. Your prefrontal cortex is acting as your brain's conductor by increasing the activity in some regions and reducing it in others. It can bring to the forefront certain activity and reduce it in other areas.

The prefrontal cortex receives connections from many brain regions and has the capacity to send signals back to these regions. This "feed-forward" and "feed-back" system enables the prefrontal cortex to monitor what's going on in the rest of the brain and based on this information send signals back to direct the volume, pacing, and rhythm of activity in specific regions. This kind of supervisory control enables the prefrontal cortex to manage and organize mental activity. We can bring to the forefront certain thoughts and keep them in mind in what psychologists call *working memory* or *short-term memory*.

Interestingly, the prefrontal cortex is the last region to develop in childhood and doesn't fully mature until after puberty (this knowledge made me a bit more sympathetic when my prepubescent sons were acting out). The prefrontal cortex is also the first cortical region to show wear and tear as we grow older. That is why one of the most significant problems in older adults is the ability to keep track of thoughts and prevent stray ones from interfering. When our executive control processes diminish we begin to have problems in focused attention, multi-tasking and inhibiting inadvertent thoughts. Thus, brain fitness as we age depends significantly on maintaining a healthy and active prefrontal cortex. The more we can engage this brain region during daily activities, the better we will be able to control our thoughts and think flexibly.

Along with the prefrontal cortex, the medial temporal lobe, which we mentioned earlier, is the second most important brain region that we depend upon for mental engagement. This brain region includes the *hippocampus*, a seahorse-shaped structure that is critical for our ability to recollect past experiences or what psychologists call *episodic memory*. Consider the following scenario: you are chatting and having a good time dining out with friends at a quaint restaurant.

During this "episode," it is your prefrontal cortex that is guiding your thoughts and actions, thus allowing you to think about what you want to order, listen to what is being said, speak coherently, and eat without getting much food on your clothes. Your brain is buzzing like crazy, as it always is, but in particular your prefrontal cortex is working to allow you to single out and focus on certain things at certain times. Throughout this event, the medial temporal cortex is linking features of this experience (sights, sounds, thoughts, feelings), as if bundling the episode as a stored time capsule. Without the medial temporal lobe these links are lost and you wouldn't be able to recollect it later as an encapsulated event.

As mentioned earlier, Alzheimer's disease damages the medial temporal cortex, which is the reason why episodic memory loss is usually one of the first symptoms. One in eight individuals 65 years and older will be diagnosed with this degenerative disease, and U.S. Census Bureau estimates that this age group will double in number during the next 20 years. It is important to keep in mind that the word *dementia* is simply a catchall term used to describe any brain disorder that causes deficits in more than one cognitive domain, such as attention, memory, and language. If you have a specific memory disorder, you have amnesia, but if you have both memory and language disorders you have dementia. With the overall U.S. population growing older, there is a pressing need for science to find ways of characterizing and preventing dementing disorders.

Biologically, Alzheimer's disease is defined by abnormal protein aggregates, known as plaques and tangles, which disrupt neural transmission. The disease typically starts in the medial temporal lobe but then spreads throughout much of the cerebral hemispheres. Early symptoms include memory impairment, particularly for recent events, but then other cognitive disorders begin to appear, such as problems in attention, language, and spatial processing. There is a genetic factor, though as with virtually all disorders, the extent to which you take care of your body influences the degree and extent of the disease.

About half the cases of dementia is caused by Alzheimer's disease. Another prevalent form is vascular or multi-infarct dementia, which is caused by fatty tissue traveling through the blood system and ultimately blocking a capillary in the brain thus preventing blood from flowing further upstream. Each time such an "infarct" (i.e., stroke) occurs, it damages brain tissue. A single infarct may not produce much or any cognitive impairment, but when they occur again and again over the span of several years, individuals end up with dementia. Vascular dementia accounts for a quarter of dementia cases. Since we know about the risk factors of cardiovascular disease (high blood pressure, high cholesterol, obesity, smoking), vascular dementia is one of the most preventable forms of dementia.

To be diagnosed as having dementia, there must be declines in several cognitive abilities to the point where you are experiencing significant mental problems, such as not remembering where you are or having difficulties handling daily activities (household chores, taking pills, financial matters). Gerontologists have formulated an intermediate or transitional state defined as *mild cognitive impairment* (*MCI*). Such individuals can still perform daily chores, but they exhibit an abnormal decline in cognition, particularly in the domain of learning and memory. Among people between the ages of 70 and 90 years, about 6% will be diagnosed with MCI. Some MCI cases will maintain the same level of impairment for many years, whereas for others it is a transitional stage toward dementia. Recent findings suggest that an early indicator of MCI is the fact that you yourself notice a dramatic change in your ability to remember recent events. In any case, if you, a family member, or friend thinks that your memory has significantly declined, a visit to your physician is advised.

Promoting Healthy Aging

So much for the bad news. Research has also shown that there are ways to promote a healthy mind and body. To begin with, it is important to realize that synaptic plasticity occurs throughout one's life (yes, you can teach old dogs new tricks). In fact, a recent study has shown that the rate of dementia in developed countries is actually decreasing in individuals over 65 years of age. This finding is attributed to the fact that we are learning how to maintain a better lifestyle, particularly through diet and exercise. Of importance is that any modification of one's behavior that promotes a physically healthy lifestyle—such as losing weight, increasing physical activity, limiting alcoholic beverages, ending a smoking or other drug habit—has profound effects on brain health and longevity.

Psychologists have considered ways to improve mental health. *Positive psychology* is a relatively new field that focuses on a science of positive subjective experience. Rather than harping on mental illness, positive psychology deals with mental fitness and ways to encourage well-being, contentment, and a satisfaction with life. This brand of psychological science has its roots in humanistic psychology, a school of psychotherapy made popular by Carl Rogers and Abraham Maslow in the 1960s. It took nearly a half century, however, to enact a scientific analysis as it is much harder to figure out how to improve wellbeing than it is to determine how it goes awry. Positive psychology seeks to change the disease-oriented nature of traditional mental health research and instead key on ways to foster wellness.

Along the lines of positive psychology, gerontologists have considered "successful aging" or how we can maintain a positive outlook throughout our lifespan. The three essential ingredients of successful aging are good physical health, enduring mental activity, and an engaging social life. One of the more provocative investigations has been the study of 678 nuns from the School Sisters of Notre Dame. Initiated by Dr. David Snowden in 1986, these nuns (75-102 years old) have been given psychological evaluations on a regular basis. Controlled living accommodations, diet, social structure, and activities make this group a fascinating one to follow. Moreover, these nuns have graciously permitted post-mortem analysis of their brains, and since the mean age of the nuns at the start of the investigation was 83 years, several pathological studies have been conducted. In one autopsy study, the degree of Alzheimer's pathology (i.e., neurofibrillary tangles) found at death was related to memory scores, even for those too early to be diagnosed with dementia. This finding suggests decrements in memory performance may be used as an early marker of the impending disease. Even more interesting, nuns who expressed positive emotions at an early age were significantly more likely to live longer!

In most aging studies, groups of older adults will perform more poorly than groups of younger adults. Yet two critical features must be kept in mind. First, the average decline across the decades of adult life is rather small, until we get to into our 60s and beyond. Second, within older age groups there is considerable variability in performance so that one can find 60- and 70-year olds who are performing as well as 20-year olds. Of course, the broad variability among older adults means that some are performing very poorly.

What accounts for variability in performance scores across older adults? Consider this rather crude analogy. Most new cars fresh out of the manufacturing plant will run rather smoothly as their engines are well oiled and the parts brand new. Now consider the performance level of a group of cars that have been on the road for 10 years. Much more variability will be observed across these cars as two critical factors will now have become very apparent. First, those that started out with more efficient parts and construction (those with better genes) will be better equipped to withstand the ravishes of normal wear and tear. Second, cars that have benefitted from being well maintained over the years (better lifestyle) will likely perform better than those not well maintained. With respect to cars and our bodies, we cannot change how we started out in the world (your genetic makeup is one case where you can definitely blame your parents); however, we can work to maintain ourselves throughout our lives.

What can we do to promote a healthy brain? It is human nature to desire the easy route—the magic pill that will melt away pounds or improve your memory. Over the decades, living through chemistry has certainly helped our well-being, but there are no quick fixes that will fight off aging completely. Indeed, drugs that facilitate memory and cognition are meant for those with debilitating disorders (i.e., dementia) and their application as a prosthetic for normal aging is not well proven. Perhaps in the future there will be drugs that will not only help us clean out our system (a liquid plumber for our brains) but will also modify the way our genes are regulated so that that they can prevent dementia or cardiovascular disease. For now, however, we are left with doing it the hard way—through ongoing care and maintenance of our physical and mental health.

Be SMART!

OK, so you've decided to break away from tired habits and enrich your brain. What now? My goal is to offer a simple proscription for a healthy mental life. It is based on psychological and brain sciences and formulated as a 5-step program. I call this program *Get SMART!* as the letters form an acronym for the five essential steps toward a healthier brain: *Get Social! Get Moving! Get Artistic! Get Responsive!* and *Get Thinking!* These steps are ordered in terms of importance. Here's your first memory aid: For the next chapter, I want you to read the headings and look at the table before your read it. This task will provide a framework for what will be discussed and will thus facilitate memory retention of the material (more on this memory aid later). By considering the five steps of *Get SMART!* I hope to engage and enrich your brain (and body) with a broad-based, multi-faceted enrichment program.

Chapter 2: Get Social!

Why Social?

You might ask yourself: if the purpose of successful aging is to keep my brain healthy, then why do I need to deal with others? It turns out that the easiest and perhaps best way to maintain a healthy brain is to *get social*. When you interact with others—with family, friends and groups—your brain becomes fully engaged. The difficulty is that as we grow older our social interactions become less frequent. We disengage from family and friends, not only by desire, but also through other circumstances, such as when family members move to another town. For many people, it is only after retirement when it becomes apparent how much our social life revolves around the office or hallway at work with fellow co-workers.

There is good news. Feelings of well-being, as indicated by ratings of self-satisfaction, actually increase with each decade between the ages of 20 and 70 years. Also, young adults tend to be happier with more peripheral friends, whereas older adults feel happier with a smaller group of close friends. Thus, our social circles tend to reduce in number, but the ones we keep become more tightly bound. Older adults also have more positive feelings about family members than do younger adults (distance makes the heart grow fonder?). Overall, even as social interactions reduce in frequency, they tend to deepen as we grow older.

The problem arises when our social network becomes so restricted that they amount to just a spouse or worse, a television. Social isolation is dangerous and considered as much a health risk as smoking, high blood pressure, or obesity. With all the comforts of home, one often avoids stepping outside the front door. Moreover, we tend to take our social interactions for granted, as if they'll always be there. Yet if your only interaction is with your spouse, what will happen when he or she dies?

The Social Brain

Freud was not too far off when he relegated humans to two essential drives—sex and aggression. Evolutionarily speaking, we are sex machines and millions of years ago a prime way of getting it was to be stronger and more aggressive than others. Of course, there are more subtle ways of attracting a mate—even during prehistoric times—such as offering a lovely string of beads to an admiring woman or praising a man for his intellect or nurturing ability. In any way it's done, your chances of passing along your genes to the next generation are much enhanced if you are adept at socially interacting with others. As a result, our brains have been built for social engagement.

Given the strong biological basis for getting social, it is not too surprising that there are universal signals that we all use to communicate our interests. You can smile at anyone anywhere in the world and that expression will be interpreted as a friendly gesture. In fact, we all should smile more frequently as the very act will induce positive feelings. Through body language and tone of voice we give out strong signals that say "please approach" or "please stay away." Often we are not even aware of eliciting such signals, yet there are basic brain mechanisms that are activated when we encourage (or discourage) social interactions.

The primitive biological system that arouses our bodies and brain begins with a small midbrain structure called the hypothalamus. It serves four basic functions that professors like to call "the four Fs"— which stands for fighting, fleeing, feeding, and mating. The hypothalamus sends out signals to the rest of the body via the pituitary gland, which releases hormones into the bloodstream. Hormones activate specific organs in the body, one of which is the adrenal gland, which releases adrenalin. Adrenalin has the effect of increasing heart rate, respiration, blood pressure, and blood sugar. This *hypothalamic-pituitary-adrenal (HPA) axis* is a general activating system that prepares the body for social engagements. It is often associated with the "fight or flight" response, though it is a general arousal mechanism that occurs during both positive and negative situations, thus allowing us to run faster, jump higher, and have sex more readily.

Activating the HPA axis on occasion is a good thing and a natural response to emotional situations. It becomes a negative factor when it is chronically activated, as in prolonged anxiety or stress, thus leading to negative long-term effects such as high blood pressure, heart attacks, strokes, and diabetes. Regulating the HPA axis—being aroused once in a while but not always—is a prime feature of healthy living. One way the hypothalamus controls this arousal system is through another biochemical, oxytocin, which inhibits activity along the HPA axis. In rodents, oxytocin contributes to a number of "prosocial" behaviors, such as mating, social bonding, anxiety reduction, and maternal attachment. The female hormone, estrogen, plays an important role in increasing the production of oxytocin, and as such, the stereotype of women being more socially attuned to emotional situations has a biological basis.

In recent years, oxytocin has been touted as the "love hormone," as a result of its relationship to romantic love, maternal bonding, and trustworthiness. In psychobiological studies, scientists have monitored levels of blood oxytocin during social engagements or administered the hormone through nasal inhalation. In one study, subjects played an investment game in which they were either "investors" or "trustees." The investor gave "money" (from 0-12 units) to an anonymous trustee, and that amount was tripled by the experimenter and given to the trustee. The trustee could keep all the money or give some of it back to the investor. When given a dose of oxytocin, investors gave more money to the trustees compared to those given a placebo, as if they had greater trust that the investor would return some funds back. Other studies have shown that prosocial behavior following a dose of oxytocin is modulated by the context or situation. For example, your sense of trust may be stronger toward compatriots with like-minded sentiments compared to those considered outside your group.

We are of course complicated beings and despite these interesting effects, oxytocin is not a love potion and won't automatically turn a lackadaisical dolt into a caring individual. All of our emotions— love, envy, jealously, pride—are driven by complex brain interactions which are dependent upon genetic predispositions, early childhood experiences, and current thoughts and feelings. Complex emotions often revolve around our ability to empathize with others. Unlike sympathy, in which we feel pity for someone, empathy is the sense of putting yourself in another's shoes. It is something like a mind meld in which we mentally transpose ourselves into another's psyche.

In 1996, the neuroscientist Giacomo Rizzolatti and colleagues discovered an interesting property of neurons in the monkey's cerebral cortex. It had been known earlier that neurons in the prefrontal cortex become active when an animal makes a motor movement, such as grabbing an object. Rizzolatti found that some neurons in this region also become active when the animal watches someone else make the same movement. These so-called *mirror neurons*

24

suggest that there are brain cells that are active when an animal is just imagining or simulating an action. Neuroimaging studies in humans have found similar "mirror-neuron" activations in a variety of brain regions, including the prefrontal cortex and the posterior parietal cortex (if you put your finger just above your ears, you'd be pointing to posterior parietal cortex).

Mirror neurons offer a neural basis for empathy. That is, when we empathize with another's plight, we imagine another's feelings. For example, put yourself in your spouse's or parents' shoes and imagine what it's like having an argument with you. You may begin to appreciate the other side of the argument (and maybe even feel the need to make an apology). If you can imagine being someone else, the posterior parietal cortex becomes particularly active. This region participates with many other brain areas and is engaged when we consider ourselves as someone else or even when we imagine ourselves in the past (reminiscing about an episodic event) or future ("what am I going to do this weekend?"). When we empathize, we also engage brain regions involved in generating emotions because we can often feel another's pleasure or pain. Interestingly, imagining the pain of others engages some of the same brain regions that are activated when we experience our own physical pain.

Through empathy we engender a sense of belongingness, because we can appreciate the similarities amongst us and garner the sense that *we're all in it together*. As social animals, we depend on this sense to feel a part of a culture or society. Thus, by affiliating with groups—that is, individuals beyond those in our household—we increase the sense of belongingness.

Engaging Yourself With Others

Psychological studies have shown the ways in which aging matures social behavior. Compared to young adults, older adults are better able to control their feelings, are less responsive to verbal attacks, and pay more attention to the positive side of life. One explanation for this maturity is that through decades of social interactions, older adults have confronted the good, bad, and ugly of how people deal with one another. As such, they better understand that choices can be made concerning how we behave and how healthy living is best achieved by focusing on the positive side of life. This positivity bias adheres to the saying, *don't sweat the small stuff,* and is important for psychological well-being as life is too short to worry about minor annoyances.

Epidemiological studies have shown that positive social engagement helps to maintain brain functions and protects against cognitive decline and dementia. The most convincing studies are long-term projects in which the same individuals are tested over many years. One study assessed 2,249 older adults (78 years or older) who were members of a health maintenance organization and free from dementing illness. They were initially surveyed on the extent of their social networks (family, friends, groups) and daily social contacts. In a follow-up analysis conducted four years later, 268 of these individuals had developed dementia. It was found that having a large social network and more daily social contacts were significant protective factors against incurring dementia, even when other factors, such as age, education, and initial health status, were controlled. Other investigations have shown that the likelihood of cognitive decline and even of dying are reduced by engaging in social activities.

How can we explain the benefits of social engagement on brain function? There are of course a variety of benefits. First, as social animals we depend on sparking that HPA arousal system, which acts to keep both our brains and bodies engaged. Second, and perhaps most important, social interactions require communication with others, which depends on comprehending and analyzing what others are saying and then making a thoughtful response. Thus, social engagement makes us *think* and be *responsive*. Third, social interactions encourage us to *move* and become physically engaged. Thus, through the simple act of interacting with others, we increase both brain and bodily activity.

There are interesting details about aging and social engagement that should considered. As indicated by the link between oxytocin and estrogen, women appear to be more responsive than men with respect to the health benefits of social engagement. Yet it is vitally important for men to consider lifelong social engagements, because older men who live alone are twice as likely to experience cognitive declines as those who live with others. Another obvious factor is that we've been assuming that your social engagements will be positive. Most will avoid negative social contact when given the choice, but there are cases, particularly with family and co-workers, when negative interactions cannot be prevented. It is not surprising that bad social engagements induce strain and anxiety, and such interactions can impair one's well-being.

We all know that particular friend who is the life of a party and has no problem chatting it up with others. Indeed, social interactions are for some as natural as breathing, and new friendships are acquired easily. For others, social interactions can be uncomfortable, difficult, or just not of interest. As mentioned earlier, when we get older, our circle of friends diminishes as we prefer to stick with long-standing, comfy relationships rather than pursue new ones. Unfortunately, this attitude can be deleterious when old friends move away, become ill, or die. When you reach the point of getting senior discounts, it becomes imperative to expand your social circle.

Making conversation is one of those things that everyone is supposed to know how to do. It's like childrearing, teaching, or remembering—some are better than others but it is assumed that everyone has the capacity to engage in such things. Yet making conversation is a skill, and all of us can learn how to improve it (the same is true for childrearing, teaching, and remembering). The website, *psychcentral.com*, includes a set of useful tips authored by Maud Purcell to help you improve your conversational skills. Some of her tips are presented below:

- ❖ **Ask a friend.** Request honest input from a trusted friend. How does she think you come across in social situations? What does she think you do well? How could you converse more effectively with others? Better yet, ask a couple of confidantes for their assessment of you.

- ❖ **Speak less and listen more.** People love to speak about themselves. In social situations, be sure to ask others about their interests, work, opinions, etc. This will take the focus off of you. A side benefit of this approach is that you will invariably be viewed as a great conversationalist, even though you've said little or nothing!

- ❖ **Keep track of new and interesting experiences.** What have you recently enjoyed? A trip to a space museum? Thai food? Your first opera? Fly-fishing? New (and attention-getting) experiences will always provide fodder for stimulating conversation.

- ❖ **Keep your own comments short and to the point.** No one is interested in hearing you drone on about your own opinions or achievements.

Brevity and humility go a long way in social situations.

It is surprising that just by listening intently and then asking pertinent questions, one can carry on an interesting and fulfilling conversation. Add some (brief) personal experiences, quips about the news (preferably avoiding politics and religion) and a little humor and one will likely be viewed as an accomplished conversationalist. As someone who often prefers to read a book rather than engage in social conversation, I have found it quite fulfilling to say "hello" to a stranger and engage in light conversation. Indeed, I have encouraged myself to do so on a daily basis.

Widening Your Social Network

With the coming of retirement—or even earlier when your children seem to have more social engagements than the Queen—make the effort to extend your own social network. The problem is that it's too easy for free time to be filled up with TV watching, playing computer games, or just mindlessly clicking links on the internet. It is not that time alone is a bad thing; it's just that it shouldn't be the only thing one does, because it can ultimately lead to complete social isolation.

Widening one's social network can be undertaken rather simply. The best routines are those that require regular time slots—daily, weekly, or otherwise scheduled dates. An easy way to set up a routine is to volunteer at a local organization, such as a school, library, community center or place of worship. Helpful hands are always needed, and volunteering engenders a sense of self-worth and accomplishment. Indeed, studies have shown that volunteering has significant effects on well-being and even delaying mortality.

I have started to volunteer at my local library where people drop off books for donation, which are then cleaned, sorted, and displayed for sale. All profits go to the library, which are rather substantial, as the bookstore is run completely by volunteers. Most importantly, I profit from regular social interactions and have the opportunity to chat about books with customers and coworkers. Community service can be quite fulfilling, and it is easy to contact your favorite organization and help out. A useful source for finding ways to volunteer is through the *AARP* (*American Association of Retire Persons*). One *AARP*-sponsored program is *Experience Corp* in which volunteers are linked to a local school and act as literacy tutors to disadvantaged young children.

Another way to develop a regular social routine is by joining a club or taking a course. In this way you can share your interests with like-minded individuals. Community centers and colleges are prime places for local club meetings and classes. Whether it's a particular hobby, artistic endeavor, music, or form of exercise, there are always groups and classes to join. If you are fortunate to live near one of the *Osher*

Lifelong Learning Institutes (*OLLI*) you have the opportunity to take interesting courses on a variety of topics. Among this semester's courses offered at my local *OLLI* is one on creative writing, one on mythology, and one on the films of Alfred Hitchcock. *OLLI* courses are taught by experts who volunteer their services, and if you feel inclined to offer a course based on your own expertise you can get involved in teaching as well. Many colleges offer similar community and continuing education courses. You will undoubtedly find a fun and socially engaging course for yourself.

Don't forget to schedule time with friends and family. Again, it is best if you can set up a regular routine—daily walks or weekly chats over tea or more potent drink. Set up your own regular group time for playing cards, having discussions (book club), or exercising (meet at the park or pool). With your spouse or friend, go out for entertainment—dinner, movie, dance, theater, sports event. I was told of a couple who had different tastes in movies and so they each wrote down a few movies they wanted to see on pieces of paper, put them in a bowl, and when it was time to go out, they'd select randomly from the bowl. One could extend this game and put all sorts of desired events in a bowl (ball game, walk in the park, movie) and play the "mystery weekend events game" with your partner. The important feature of this game is to guarantee that every weekend you'll get out of house and away from habitual duties.

Baby boomers are the last generational group who grew up before personal computers were invented. With email service available in the 1990s, search engines (*Yahoo*, *Google*) becoming popular in the early 2000s, and social media, such as *Facebook* and blogging sites, arriving a half-decade later, anyone currently in or approaching retirement learned computer skills during their adult years. Indeed, many baby boomers still have difficulty dealing with computers, electronic tablets, and smartphones (not to mention remote controls). It is, however, as necessary to know how to access the World Wide Web for social engagements as it was necessary to have a phone prior to the internet revolution.

Some may feel that computers and smartphones are diminishing our capacity for social interactions. Yet I would contend that their use has the potential of keeping us more socially engaged with friends and family. With *Facebook*, for example, I am exceedingly familiar with the on-goings of friends and family. The information can be over-whelming (note to friends: I'd rather not know if you had a café latte today or that you are stepping on a plane to Anaheim). Through computer interactions, we can keep "in touch" with friends who you may not have seen for decades, yet still have a fondness for those good ol' days in college or high school. With a click of a button, posted photos allow you to share events with family and friends who live hundreds or thousands of miles away. Findings suggest that the greater use of social networks and number of friends in your internet circle is related to greater positive feeling and perceived social support.

Social networking sites offer the opportunity to arrange actual meetings with friends and family. Moreover, it is easy to find out online when local clubs and classes meet. There are social meeting sites such as *meetup.com*, which list numerous clubs and events in your locale. Just clicking on this site, I see that within 10 miles of me I can join clubs with individuals interested in such diverse activities as yoga, photography, volleyball, writing, hiking, dining, and karaoke. If you are not comfortable with the use of computers, electronic tablets, or e-readers, I strongly encourage you to get comfy and take class or ask a friend to assist you to become computer-savvy.

Get It On!

Family and friends—they are the lifeblood of successful aging. As we age, we need to make a concerted effort to maintain (and hopefully extend) social networks. Volunteer your services, take a course, join a club, schedule regular dates with family and friends, use the internet to engage with others— make the effort and consciously work on creating new social engagements. There is a snowball effect in getting social—as you develop more friends, you soon realize you are engaging with friends of friends, who may ultimately become part of your "best friends" circle. The important point is that there is now substantial evidence that those with enriched social networks, are happier, more cognitively intact, and live longer. As such, the absolute most important step in successful aging and a healthy brain is to **get social**.

Get Social!

Volunteer	Work at a school, library, community center, or place of worship.
Take a Class	Learn a new hobby, subject matter, or language.
Chat it Up	Schedule time for friends and family, meals, cards/games, "tea" time.
Make a Date	Go to the movies, theater, ball game, other entertaining event.
Network	Interact through social media, such as Facebook and blogs.

Chapter 3: Get Moving!

Successful aging of mind and body go hand in hand. Unfortunately, as we age those aches and pains tend to increase, as do those mental lapses, such as opening your refrigerator door and asking, "Now what did I come here for?" Over the past several decades scientific investigations have advanced our understanding of how our bodies and brains age, and more importantly how we can reduce the negative impact of aging. The bottom line is that it's time for action, because an essential step toward a healthy lifestyle is to *get moving!*

Imagine your circulatory system as extensive plumbing, and you begin to appreciate the importance of keeping those pipes free of grit and corrosion. Moreover, even though your brain amounts to only 2% of your body in weight, as much as 25% of the blood that flows out of your heart is pumped directly to it. This disproportionate flow is due to the fact that there is little capacity for your brain to store energy as fat, and thus it's vital for blood flow to provide a continuous supply of nutrients—especially oxygen and glucose. If you fail to get blood to your brain, as in a heart attack, you will lose consciousness in 10 seconds, and after 5 to 10 minutes you will likely incur permanent brain damage. Thus, anything that keeps your plumbing clear, in particular physical exercise, will disproportionately impact on brain health.

Physical activity is also important for maintaining your natural body rhythms. Our bodies are designed to expend energy during the day and sleep during the night. In fact, restful sleep is benefitted by physical exertion during the day. Exercise also helps in regulating brain chemicals, which can reduce and even aid in preventing depressive illness. These days, the problem with everyday activities is that they tend not to depend on physical activity. Whether at work or in retirement, an extraordinary amount of time is spent immobile as we look at a screen, read text, or just sit around. Eons ago, primitive humans spent most of their time up and about simply to survive, and only a few generations ago most people engaged in rather extensive physical labor during the day. Our physiology is geared toward daily physical activity, and these days it is crucial to replace those ancestral necessities of physical activity with "voluntary" exercise. We must satisfy the body's expectation to exert energy and replace hunting, gathering, and farming with walking, biking, and swimming.

Healthy Bodies, Healthy Brains

The problem with getting old is that over time we simply experience wear and tear. Even individuals who are in good physical health will experience some age-related changes. In a recent study, a select group of exceptionally healthy older adults were given a series of physical and mental tests. These individuals were active recreational cyclists aged 55 to 79 years who did not smoke and were free of cardiovascular or hypertensive disease. As expected, these fit individuals scored extremely well on all physiological and cognitive measures and often showed no aging effects within the group. Although young adults were not assessed, it is likely that these older adults could outperform many 20-year olds on these fitness measures. There were, however, some significant aging effects, most notably on measures of oxygen uptake, muscular strength, and bone density. Thus, significant health improvements will occur with continued physical activity, yet it is likely that as we enter our 70s and 80s, we'll still incur some slowing, aches, and pains.

Research investigations by Dr. Arthur Kramer and colleagues at the University of Illinois, Urbana-Champaign have provided some of the most informative findings concerning the effects of exercise on the brain. In one study, groups of 60- and 70-year olds were randomly assigned to one of two exercise programs. One group engaged in aerobic exercises for six months in which they focused on increasing heart rate during training (e.g., treadmill walking). The other group engaged in a stretching and toning program. Physiological measures and brain MRI scans were taken before and after training. Compared to the stretching and toning group, the aerobic group showed improved oxygen intake suggesting overall increases in cardiovascular fitness. In addition, the aerobic group showed increased brain volume in the frontal and temporal cortices as well as larger white matter tracts. These findings are significant as they showed that 60-70 year olds exhibited healthier brain measures even when aerobic exercise was initiated later in life.

In a follow-up study, older adults were assigned to a one-year training program of either treadmill walking or stretching. Measures of fMRI functional connectivity—that is, how well brain areas exhibit coordinated activity—showed that aerobic exercise increased the degree to which the frontal, temporal and parietal cortices work together. This finding is interesting because these brain regions give us higher cognitive functioning, such as executive control and goal planning. Other investigations have shown that physical activity can also benefit learning and memory ability.

It was long supposed that after puberty very little brain plasticity occurred. Once you hit that developmental point, the common lore was that brain growth stopped and it was only degradation from then on. Yet recent advances in neurobiology have shattered that myth, as there are certain regions in the brain where neurogenesis—the birth of new neurons—occurs throughout the life span. One highly plastic region is the dentate gyrus, which is particularly interesting because it is in the medial temporal lobe and works with the hippocampus to establish new memories. Animal studies have shown that these new dentate gyrus neurons become functionally active during learning and memory tasks. Even more important, enriching one's lifestyle, both physically and mentally, increases the number of neurons that are born in the dentate gyrus and helps to integrate them into new memory circuits, even in later life. Neuroimaging studies in humans have shown that the hippocampal region increases in size following aerobic exercise programs (treadmill walking, stationary bicycling).

There are studies in which participants learn new material while exercising. One study had participants ride a stationary bicycle while at the same time learning new vocabulary words. On the following day, those who were learning while cycling performed better than those who were learning in the normal fashion, while sitting. An additional group was included who cycled just before learning but was sitting during learning. This group performed as well those who learned while exercising, but their performance was rather variable. I do know of young professors who have replaced the standard office chair and desk with treadmills and standing platforms for their computers. Such workplace transformations can have great benefits for physical health as merely standing is better than sitting all day. Whether one should actually exercise while learning may depend on the degree to which the exercise requires mental effort. We know that multitasking is not optimal for attention, and if you have to monitor your exercise or if you're too exhausted to think, it may be better to separate physical activity from mental concentration.

Several studies do suggest that aerobic exercise just prior to learning will facilitate long-term memory. The neuroscientist Wendy Suzuki conducted a study in which her undergraduate NYU class participated in one hour of aerobic exercise before class. At the end of the semester these students performed better on a pattern memory task compared to students taking the same course but without the pre-lecture aerobics. It is, however, not clear whether improvements from exercise specifically improved memory for the lecture material itself. However, other studies suggest that aerobic exercise just prior to learning will facilitate long-term memory for the specific material learned.

With respect to preventative measures, large-scale investigations have shown that Alzheimer's Disease and overall mortality rates can be forestalled by regular exercise. In one study, 4,311 males aged 52 to 72 were evaluated on their physical activity and re-assessed 12-14 years later. There was a clear protective benefit of exercise as death rates more than doubled for those who rated themselves as inactive compared to those who said they engaged in moderate activity. Moreover, inactive men who then increased their physical activity exhibited a significant drop in mortality rates compare to inactive men who continued their sedentary lifestyle. Similarly, individuals with mild cognitive impairment appeared to show benefits from a daily exercise program, specifically in factual knowledge. Thus, not only will physical activity increase longevity, it has potential benefits in staving off or reducing the impact of dementia.

Getting Physical: How Much and What Kind?

Some of you baby boomers might remember the Olivia Newton John song that included the phrase, "let's get physical," which was of course a euphemism for engaging in torrid sex. Well, if that's the way you want to get moving, it's fine by me. Yet it would be useful to set out some basic guidelines regarding the extent and type of physical activities that will yield the greatest benefit for brain health. As shown by many studies, aerobic exercise is by far the most important thing. There is also evidence suggesting resistance training (e.g., weights, yoga) will keep your muscles supple, which will reduce age-related aches and pains.

The *Centers for Disease Control and Prevention* offer guidelines for adults 65 years and older who are generally fit. Ideally, you should engage in *moderate-intensity aerobic* activity for at least 2½ hours per week (e.g., every day for 20-25 min) and do *muscle-strengthening* exercises on two (or more) days per week. The aerobic exercise should get your heart pumping but not so hard that you can't converse comfortably (5 or 6 on a scale where 10 is most out of breath). A hardy walk, bike, or swim should do the trick as will active group activities, such as tennis, golf, or dancing.

Muscle strengthening and toning exercises can involve weights, calisthenics (sit-ups, push-ups), elastic bands, or yoga. Such exercises should work all major muscle groups, including legs, hips, back, abdomen, chest, shoulders, and arms. Be sure to include stretching exercises with muscle strengthening ones, as these tend to keep your joints flexible and reduce those common aches and pains associated with a stiff back or painful shoulder or knee. If you are starting out from a rather sedentary lifestyle, it is important to initiate these programs gradually and seek a physician's advice if concerned about your capabilities.

For those who seek more vigorous physical activities, such as jogging, aerobic dancing or more intensive cycling or swimming, the *Centers for Disease Control and Prevention* advice is at least 1¼ hours per week (10-15 min daily) of vigorous-intensity aerobic activity and 2 or more days of muscle-strengthening activities. Such aerobic exercises will put you out of breath momentarily, so you'll have to pause between breaths to talk (7 or 8 on a scale of 10). Of course a mixture of moderate to more vigorous activities is useful, particularly in keeping the training varied.

In addition to the general importance of aerobic exercise for brain health, should one find a regime that combines exercise with learning? As mentioned above, there is evidence for the benefits of exercising before, during, and after learning, though it appears optimal to engage in aerobic exercise just before learning. When you pump up just before a mental task, you prime the brain with increased blood flow, which if anything else will give your entire brain an enriched setting for mental concentration. Given that there are memory-related brain processes that are engaged just after learning, in particular hippocampal activity, exercising just after a learning event may be beneficial. However, if you do that alone, you will not reap the benefits of an exercised-primed brain during learning. Thus, my suggestion would be that just before you engage in a mental task (e.g., just before a class, a reading assignment, or writing a book chapter), it would be beneficial to perform a few minutes of aerobic exercise (e.g., jumping jacks). If you also want to exercise afterwards, go for it.

Regardless of the activity, the most important thing is to keep at it. Motivation is key, and if your routine is too strenuous, tedious, or just not fun, then it's time to change the program. With any exercise routine, you must avoid over-exerting your muscles and work up gradually to a desired amount of activity. Once you find a regular routine that you enjoy, I find it useful to mark a set time of the day for 30-40 minutes of physical activity. Another way to avoid making exercise tedious is to join a sports club or schedule regular activities with friends or family. In this way, one combines getting social with getting moving. If you prefer social interaction with someone who doesn't talk back to you, you may prefer to take daily strolls with a pet dog.

Learning New Tricks

Consider Olga Kotelko who became interested in track and field at age 77. Not having participated in any such events she began training with a coach for Masters competitions. Three years later she competed in the World Championships and won six gold medals and broke several world records in such events as the hammer throw, javelin, high jump, and 200-meter run. Olga continued her training and over the next 15 years she won 750 gold medals and had broken over 30 world records. She died in 2014 at age 95, just months after competing in the World Masters Championships and setting new records for her age group. Olga's accomplishments are extraordinary considering she began her training at an age when most of us would be grunting just to crawl out of bed. She stands as evidence for the notion that you can learn new tricks in your 70s and beyond. Indeed, taking up physical activity in later life and keeping at it on a regular basis acts significantly to improve one's physical and mental health.

In addition to encouraging us to explore new skills in later life, Olga's success provides important evidence for two other points. First, it is extremely useful to have an instructor or trainer to assist you in the proper ways to develop a skill. More importantly a coach can give you personal feedback and correct mistakes. Olga hired a personal trainer, which is ideal, though taking a sports class—such as in tennis, golf, swimming or bowling—will significantly help to sharpen and develop psychomotor skills. Regular sessions in class or with a personal trainer will keep motivation up and encourage daily exercise.

A second lesson learned from Olga's success is to understand one's limitations. As mentioned earlier, regardless of how fit you are, during your 60s and 70s you will undoubtedly incur loss of muscle mass and reduced metabolic efficiency (e.g., oxygen intake). You should engage in physical activity often, though keep in mind not to over exert yourself. Olga said: "If you undertrain, you might not finish. If you overtrain, you might not start." Indeed, over extending oneself can be deleterious both physically and mentally. It is key to maintain a healthy physical routine, yet still keep in mind that the muscles and bones are not what they used to be. Everyone needs to appreciate their own limitations and to feel good about what they can do rather than ruminate over what they cannot do.

Scientific investigations have shown that there are better ways of acquiring a new sports skill than what was once thought. For instance, when we practice a skill there is a tendency to focus on a specific part of the skill then move on to another part. This form of blocking one's practice might proceed as working on your tennis backhand or golf putting for a period of time, then moving onto some other aspect of the sport. It turns out that this kind of blocked training is not as effective as mixing things up by varying what you practice during your training session. In one of my favorite sports skills experiment, baseball players from the Cal Poly San Luis Obispo team were divided into two groups of batting practice regimes: one group trained in a blocked fashion so that the batters were pitched 15 fastballs in a row, 15 curveballs, and then 15 change ups. The other group was given a variable training in which each batter was given the same 45 pitches but they were intermixed and randomly sequenced. During early practice sessions the blocked group did hit the ball better than the group given variable training. However, six weeks after training, the batters given variable practice hit the ball better than those given blocked practice, *even when they were tested using blocked sets.* The advantage of variable practice has been replicated with a variety of skills, including basketball, badminton, typing, and even bean bag throwing in children.

There are several reasons for the effectiveness of varying the training session even though blocking one's practice might feel like a better method. First, the early benefits of blocked practice gives us a sense that there's improvement. This early feedback encourages us to repeat the action to "get it right." In varied practice you don't have the advantage of back-to-back repetitions, and thus the task is more attention demanding as we must reset our muscles each time to prepare for a different psychomotor skill (e.g., backhand, forehand, serve). It is the very fact that we must attend each time that ultimately produces the benefits of varied practice. Under a blocked practice regime, such as practicing twenty backhand shots in a row, our muscles have a short-term memory of what we've just done. If we have just succeeded in hitting the backhand, we simply mimic that same movement without much thought or attention to what we're doing. Varied practice requires us to maintain attention every time and to work on developing the rather broad vocabulary of psychomotor responses needed in any complex skill. Thus, for efficient skill learning, mix it up and vary the skills set during each practice session.

When learning a skill, we need to make subtle muscle adjustments and coordinate our movements. We learn what is successful through immediate feedback—seeing if our tennis serve is in bounds, if our tee shot stays in the fairway, or if we manage not to step on someone's foot during the tango. An instructor or trainer assists by noting what adjustments need to be made. Skill learning is rather special in that it requires repetitive practice to coordinate the muscles and have them do what we want them to do. Thus, a person given a basketball for the first time can't be expected to make consistent free throws. For any complex skill, it is best to learn gradually and not make things overly difficult. Interestingly, as much as skill learning requires thought and attention during practice, it can be deleterious to your skill during a game. That is, you don't want to be thinking about what little muscle adjustments you need to make when playing in a game. Instead, you should just let your muscles enact the successful procedure you had acquired during practice. Practice requires tinkering, attending, and adjusting your muscle movements, but once you're in the game, on the dance floor, or in any competition, it is better to turn off your thought processes and "let the force be with you."

Keep At It!

When it comes down to a daily routine for exercise or for anything perceived as a "routine," the primary concern is *motivation*. Just the notion of a routine suggests something that is somewhat arduous or less enticing to do without some kind of incentive—would you consider having to partake in a daily serving of dessert or glass of wine a *routine*? In other words, for many individuals it will take mental effort and a commitment to exercise on a daily basis. If so, then let the incentive be good health, fewer aches and pains, prevention from disease, and most importantly more efficient brain functioning. For things that we feel we *ought* to do, it is expected that our motivation will have its ups and downs.

Once you do get moving, a great way to motivate yourself is to keep a daily record of your activities. You'll soon notice improvements along the way, such as being able to walk, swim, or jog farther with less exertion. There are now activity monitors that you can wear on your belt or wrist that will automatically record your daily steps and other movements. You can also obtain apps for your smartphone to monitor and record daily activity. Attending to such logs acts as a reminder of your need for daily physical activity and will encourage you to keep at it. Just as it is important to move for a healthy brain, you'll need to invoke some mental effort to keep moving.

Psychologists will tell you the best motivator is intrinsic. That is, the drive to get moving should come from within rather than from someone (like me) telling you what you ought to do. You can be intrinsically motivated for long-term gains, such for better physical and mental health in the future, yet the best way to keep moving is to find ways to make your physical activity immediately enjoyable. Mix it up with a variety of activities or find ways to make your exercising less of a routine. Join a sports club, class, or dance group, which will allow you to meet others with similar interests. Let the fun be in the doing and you'll automatically reap the benefits of good health.

Some of us are goal-oriented and enjoy the commitment required to accomplish tasks we set for ourselves. I do not consider myself as an intensely goal-directed individual, but one year, after decades of swimming for exercise and enjoyment, I set a goal for myself to partake in the *Escape From Alcatraz Sharkfest* event. As the name implies, hundreds of individuals are taken out to Alcatraz Island, site of the famed high-security prison, where they jump off a ferryboat and swim the 1.25 miles to San Francisco, though to date no sharks have been sighted. During the months before the event, I found myself training as I never had since my days on the high school swim team. The excitement and joy of being in the middle of the San Francisco bay was extraordinary and rather surreal. It is a memory that I'll always cherish. Such goals act as milestones that we know are challenging to reach but stir us both physically and mentally. They help motivate us to move more and practice harder. So, I encourage such goal-oriented initiatives—sign up for a running, biking, or swimming event (or do all three in a triathlon), take part in a tennis or golf tournament, join a sports team. Importantly, the goal one should consider with such undertakings should be to strive for a personal best rather than feel as if we have to compete to be better than everyone else, particularly because in any competition, there is only person who achieves that goal.

There is a PBS series entitled *Sacred Journeys* which comprised of six pilgrimages, including religious treks to Mecca in Saudi Arabia, Lourdes in France, and Kumbh Mela in India. The particular episode that captured my attention was the Buddhist pilgrimage on the Japanese island of Shikoku, in which one visits 88 temples situated around the island's perimeter. My mother was born on Shikoku, and I had heard of relatives who had taken the journey, mainly by bus, though in ancient times, and even now each year, people have trekked on foot the 750 mile path to the temples. What makes these journeys enticing is the combination of spiritual and physical involvement. Interestingly, many who were interviewed in the program were not practicing Buddhists, Muslims, Catholics, or Hindis. These individuals decided to participate in a pilgrimage for their own personal spiritual growth. I find it interesting that such undertakings interlace physical and spiritual goals and together foster an improved body and mind. It is enticing for me to imagine going to Shikoku and walking the entire route. Yet one doesn't have to partake in any of these specific journeys. Instead, one could create personal pilgrimage—walk or bike as far as you can from your home in a day or designate a lake or coastline for an extensive swim. Make the event both a physical and mindful experience.

After I retired from my faculty position at UC Berkeley, I moved to Oahu to enjoy the island's environs and begin my new career as a freelance writer. The Shikoku pilgrimage gave me an idea, which I realized late in 2015. I decided to take a walk around the island. Oahu's perimeter is roughly 150 miles and largely accessible through coastal roads and beaches. It was my intent to walk on the beach as much as possible, though doing this was much harder than walking along the road. They say that Eskimos have dozens of words for "snow." I developed my own set of terms for "sand" (*squeaky, mushy, angled, impossible*).

I am by no means the sort of athlete who would find this kind of excursion a simple jaunt. I more resemble Bill Bryson's physique as portrayed in his wonderful book, *A Walk in the Woods*. I decided to appreciate my limitations and set rest days between daily hikes. For most of my pilgrimage, I was able to drive or bus to the previous day's endpoint, walk my 10-15 miles, then take a bus back home or back to my car. In preparation of each day's hike, I learned about the geography, culture, and history of each region. The experience was extraordinarily life fulfilling as it gave me an unique introduction to my new environs. Also, I have never before understood physical exhaustion as I did after walking 15 miles in humid 90 degree and.

Highly skilled athletes, as well musicians, will tell you that on occasion they achieve a peak experience often described as being "in the zone" or "in the groove." Likewise, marathon runners and long-distance swimmers talk about achieving a "second wind" in the middle of a race. At such times, these athletes feel so attuned to the moment that physical exertion or duress are non-existent. The psychologist Mihaly Csikszentmihalyi characterizes such optimally pleasurable experiences as *flow*. He defines this experience as a heightened focusing of attention, a merging of awareness and action, a loss of time, and a clear sense of goals. A key feature is what he calls *autotelic quality*, which he defines as a sense of satisfaction for no other reason than feeling the pleasures of the activity. Flow can be achieved during many activities, including physical activity (sports, dance), artistic performance (music, art), and even purely mental activity (science, math). The experience of flow once again affirms the overwhelmingly positive experience one attains by a heightened sense of both body and mind.

So get moving! Remember your entire brain will benefit from pumping more blood to it. Schedule aerobic workouts on a regular basis. Make it fun by moving with friends, taking a class, or working with a trainer. It is difficult to get moving when you are experiencing those aches and pains from rusty joints and muscles. Flex those joints with stretching exercises every day and strengthen your muscles with restraint exercises (weight training, calisthenics, yoga). Get out there and learn a new sports skill or dance. Mix it up, have fun, and get social while you're moving your body!

Get Moving!

Off Your Duff	Walk, jog, swim, bike, dance...get your heart pumping!
Muscle Tone	Weights, calisthenics, gym, yoga; reduce those aches and pains.
Take a Walk	Get a dog, stroll the neighborhood, park further away.
Brain Warm-up	Five min aerobics just before reading, writing, a class, or other mindful event.
Social Workout	Set a regular exercise date with a friend, family member, or coach.

Chapter 4: Get Artistic!

So you're getting social and starting to move, now why would artistic expression be the next step toward a healthy brain? It turns out that exercising your creative side—and we all have one—activates broad brain networks in a rather unique fashion. When we think artistically we engage ourselves fully by combining perceptions, thoughts, and feelings in new and different ways. Art forces our brains to restructure thought and make new connections. So stir those creative juices and *get artistic*.

The Creative Mind

Creativity is often described as the ability to produce a work that is both novel and useful. We tend to apply the term to society's geniuses, but of course creative acts occur every day—from a twist on an old recipe, a clever idea, or even a funny joke—and we will include these common portrayals in our initiative to *get artistic*. Like so many other psychological concepts, such as intelligence or memory, creativity is not a single entity. The product of creativity should be new and different, but of course not any crazy idea is a creative one. Creative works have a purpose—they change the way we think or feel about the world.

Some people seem to have an uncanny way of working "out of the box" and coming up with remarkably interesting ways of doing things. Whether in art, music, sports, science, technology or business, it takes both exceptional genes and extensive training to become the Picasso, Curie, or Jobs in your field. Yet we all can and should strive to be creative. What does that actually entail? Scientific studies on the nature of creativity have focused on several themes. One is *divergent thinking*, the ability to conjure up many novel solutions to a problem. A common application of divergent thinking is *brainstorming*, those group sessions in which individuals try to derive many possible answers to a posed question, even if they seem far-fetched at first. Linus Pauling, the noted scientist and winner of two Nobel Prizes, said: "The best way to have a good idea is to have a lot of ideas, and throw away the bad ones." One must be open to conjuring up thoughts and linking them in novel ways. A psychological test of divergent thinking asks individuals to come up with as many uses for a particular object (e.g., brick, paper clip) as possible.

Divergent thinking is less a part of our everyday mental life because our brains are geared toward converging on tried and true pathways. The outside world is so full of regularities, such as the way light reflects off objects, the sound of raindrops, and the taste of sweet fruit, that our brains interpret these sensations quickly and without much thought. Likewise, we know immediately when we need a brick or a paper clip, so why think of alternate uses? In a stable environment, our brain's response to everyday regularities works just fine. There are, however, times when we need to adjust to environmental changes and find alternate solutions, such as when a hammer is not available. In these times divergent thinking is required.

Creative individuals notice things that others ignore or deem irrelevant. We discussed in Chapter 1 the role of the prefrontal cortex in guiding our thoughts while filtering out distractions. Without such supervision, we are subject to mind wandering. With respect to creativity, one could imagine that *turning off one's prefrontal cortex* may actually facilitate divergent thinking. That is, de-focusing our thoughts and letting our brain wander a bit may entice new and unusual ideas to bubble up into consciousness. In fact, brain imaging studies have shown that reduced prefrontal function is conducive to divergent thinking. Also, patients with a disease called frontotemporal dementia develop interests in artistic expression. It is not that these individuals are creating world renowned artworks. Instead, they have a newfound desire to express themselves artistically, which may be related to a lack of filtering or regulating emotions. Thus, by relaxing our need to converge on familiar solutions— that is by easing up on prefrontal control—we may allow divergent ideas and associations to enter consciousness.

Creativity is more than divergent thinking as one must ultimately hone in on an innovative or useful idea. When we think of genius inventions, there is often a simplicity to them that we typically characterize as *insightful* or *elegant*. We may even ask ourselves, "Why didn't I think of that?" Creative solutions often occur after much rumination, as if they needed to incubate before being hatched. Sometimes, they seem to occur spontaneously like a cartoon "light bulb" moment when a fresh idea just pops into mind. Regardless of the speed with which creative inspirations occur, they are all products of expert knowledge and superb technical skill. Innovators use their knowledge as the source of the bits and pieces that when put together form a creative idea. A worthy example is Steve Jobs who found ways of putting knowledge and technologies that were already out there and packaging them in novel ways to create the *Mac*, *iPod*, and *iPhone*.

Consider the stand-up comedian or jazz musician who must spontaneously sequence pieces of knowledge together to create a novel performance. Such feats cannot be accomplished without a vast database and a free-wheeling (i.e., divergent) ability to tap into it. Likewise, creative minds must be able to hold many thoughts in mind and flexibly move between them. As mentioned earlier, our ability to hold things in mind depends on the prefrontal cortex, which engages working memory processes that allow us to maintain and manipulate thoughts in short-term memory. In neuroimaging studies, creative individuals on certain occasions show heightened activity in the prefrontal cortex. This finding may seem at odds with the idea that creativity depends on turning off one's prefrontal cortex. It appears that divergent thinking depends on shutting off the prefrontal cortex, whereas focusing in on a particularly innovative thought amongst the many divergent ones requires the prefrontal cortex. Thus, the key to creativity is a flexible de-focusing and re-focusing of one's thoughts. One needs to rapidly shut off and turn on one's prefrontal cortex, which may be the reason why creativity is not such a commonplace occurrence. As suggested by the Linus Pauling quote, it is important to generate many ideas *and* focus in on the good ones.

Innovative thinking depends on having a global or big picture perspective. We often associate this notion with being imaginative, which is interesting as it connotes a visual or spatial process. The ability to think spatially is helpful in seeing the big picture—the forest rather than the trees. One aspect of creative thinking is the ability to make metaphorical connections, such as when Einstein considered how light would be viewed on a speeding train compared to on a platform. His linking of the speed of light with a speeding train helped him to develop his theory of relativity. Psychologists use the *Remote Associates Test* to assess this ability to make analogical connections. Subjects are given three words, such as *river, note, account,* and must find a single word that is associated with all three (i.e., bank). A somewhat harder one is what word is related to *cross, rain,* and *tie?*

A general myth about creativity is that it is primarily a right-brain phenomenon. It is true that the two cerebral hemispheres are predisposed to process information differently, most notably verbal information being processed in the left hemisphere and spatial information being processed in the right hemisphere. Yet there is significant crosstalk between hemispheres and aspects of language and spatial function are processed in the non-dominant side. It is also true that the left hemisphere is biased toward processing detailed or local information, whereas the right hemisphere is biased toward global information. As creative individuals are often viewed as imaginative (perhaps spatially minded) and seeing the big picture (perhaps globally minded), the right hemisphere has been interpreted as the sole source of creativity. Yet, it is certainly the case that many regions—located in the left, right, front, and back of the brain—contribute to mental processes involved in being creative. These processes support divergent thinking, rapid access to knowledge, cognitive flexibility, technical skill, and imaginative thinking.

In a fascinating set of studies, Charles Limb and colleagues investigated brain activity while musicians improvised. In one study, jazz pianists were placed in an fMRI scanner and asked to improvise at times and at other times play a memorized piece. When they were improvising, sensory and language areas were highly activated, whereas regions in the prefrontal cortex were deactivated, as if the freeing of executive control was important for rapid associative thoughts. There was, however, a region in the prefrontal cortex—the most anterior part of the brain known as the frontal polar cortex—which was highly active during improvisation. This region is associated with higher-order goals and plans related to maintaining a general conceptual point or theme. Improvisation seems to require the maintenance of overarching ideas or moods that must move flexibly from one to another. Similar findings of activations and de-activations have been observed in freestyle rappers.

In summary, when we think creatively, we release ourselves from familiar ways and attitudes. We open our brains to divergent thoughts that otherwise would not have come to mind. We must think flexibly, which allows us to piece together the good bits of divergent thoughts and toss out the bad ones. Inquisitiveness and imagination are also key factors. Creating art—and I mean this in the broadest sense from visual arts, music, dance, cooking, invention, and just being imaginative in our daily lives—provides the opportunity to engage our brain in new and exciting ways while releasing us from the regular and mundane.

Beholding Art

Mark Rothko, the 20th century abstract painter, placed broad strokes of color on canvas to make the beholder feel the same "basic human emotions—tragedy, ecstasy, doom" that he felt while painting. Keith Jarrett, the renowned jazz pianist, claimed that when he improvises on stage his "main job is listening." These two artists understood the close bond between creating art and beholding it. Be it at an art gallery, movie theater, musical performance, or in your home watching TV or surfing the web, when we experience another's creative work, we resonate with the artist. Indeed, beholding art has the potential to heighten our senses, fill us with emotions, and think about the world in new and different ways.

In the past several years I have become interested in the ways we experience art. I use the plural form, "ways," because there is not a single art experience, as we can appreciate art from many perspectives. Based on a long standing Western view—established by thoughtful 18th century philosophers, *art is only for art's sake*—that is, for no other reason than to instill an emotional experience of beauty or awe. This *aesthetic* response in its most heightened sensation gives us that "wow" feeling, experienced perhaps in the presence of Michelangelo's David or while listening to a Beethoven quartet. I will not deny such emotional responses, yet I feel that our experience with art can be appreciated in other ways. For instance, art can teach us to understand the world in different ways. It can elicit a myriad of feelings outside of beauty and awe—such as surprise, fear, anger, and even disgust. Art often reminds us of the past—our personal history as well as cultural history.

I have characterized the relation between artist and beholder with a simple framework that I call the I-

SKI model. The acronym highlights the artist's *intention* to create an artwork and the beholder's mental experience of driving *sensations, knowledge,* and *emotions*. Many acknowledge that sensations and emotions are part of our art experience, yet we don't always appreciate how much knowledge contributes to this experience. In fact, our appreciation of art depends significantly on what we know—from everyday knowledge about the world, from our cultural experiences, and from personal encounters. We don't always consider the role of knowledge, because the *art for art's sake* view suggests that an artwork should strike our emotions directly without any thoughts. Actually, those so-called "direct" responses are largely driven by what we know. Even basic things like the foods we like, the colors we prefer, the music that turns us on, are driven largely by past experiences.

We can grasp the importance of knowledge in driving our art experience when we say that we like something but "it's an acquired taste"—such as the appeal of bebop jazz, abstract art, or sushi. The history of art is fraught with examples of changes in preferences or styles, and often new works are viewed as so perverse that their very status as "art" is questioned. Incredibly, this sentiment was true for *Impressionist* paintings, which when first viewed were considered by many as ugly and crude. With our 21st century eyes and brains, those sentiments seem so utterly off base as we now see beauty and grace in the same works. It is, however, not uncommon these days to overhear at a contemporary art museum a person saying to another, "Is that really art?"

Clearly, what we know determines what we like. New works may appear odd or distasteful at first because we cannot easily incorporate them into our knowledge base. Daniel Berlyne, a psychologist who studied aesthetic responses, argued that our art experience is driven by novelty, surprise, and incongruity. He suggested that there's a sweet spot with respect to our consideration of art, in that works that are somewhat novel or incongruous are interesting but too much of these things can lead to a negative reaction. For some new works of art, if it's way out, we won't understand it and may even find it distasteful. The opposite of newness is of course familiarity, and thus more exposure and experience with an artistic style could bring us to enjoy further variations more fully. The important point is that our appreciation of art broadens with familiarity and the more we know the greater the possibility that an artwork will lie in our "sweet spot" of appreciation. With respect to musical trends—such as bebop, rock, and rap—one generation's "noise" is another's anthem to life.

Even though our appreciation of art is based on knowledge and thought, we can still partake in emotional pleasures. Based on my I-SKE framework, a full art experience occurs when our sensations, knowledge, *and* emotions are all driven to the max. I remember having a "wow" moment when standing in front of Van Gogh's *Starry Night Over The Rhone* when it was on display at the deYoung Museum in San Francisco. I experienced such intense feelings that nothing seemed to exist except me and the painting. Such moments are often accompanied by goose bumps or chills up the spine. In brain imaging studies, Robert Zatorre and colleagues had subjects listen to their favorite piece of music. When individual reported "chills up the spine" a network of brain areas was activated which is associated with emotional pleasure and reward.

If such moments were the only reason for experiencing art, then I would be sadly disappointed, because those events for me are few and far between. By considering other ways to appreciate art, I can open myself to various experiences—in particular a *learning* experience. When I look at art I try to relate a work to my own personal background or knowledge. From this perspective, I may develop a conceptual sense of how an artwork relates to its historical setting—that is the nature of the artist and the cultural context in which the artwork was created. We can imagine how an artwork tells a story about life, culture, or the art experience itself. We may want to consider further and learn about the social or political events surrounding the artist. In this way beholding art enables one to learn about the world and experience life through another's creative output. As a learning experience, whenever I go to an art museum, I spend a good deal of time reading the information printed on the gallery walls and the little cards that identify the artist and other information about the artwork, such as when and where it was created.

As described by the quotes of Rothko and Jarrett, creating art and beholding it go hand in hand. As such, one can gain a better appreciation of artistic expression with familiarity in how a work is created. As mentioned earlier, I have an interest in photography and during my 40s I took workshops to hone my skills. My favorite workshop was attended in the late 1990s when I spent several days with Cole Weston, a professional art photographer who is more notably known as the son of Edward Weston. Edward Weston changed the way we look at photographs by depicting simple objects, such as a seashell or vegetable, and making us see them as abstract images of lines, shadings, and textures. At the workshop, I learned techniques of shooting, developing, and printing but most importantly learned much about Edward Weston himself as we visited his home in Carmel, California where his grandson, Kim Weston, now lives. As I have developed my own skills in photography and learned more about its history, I feel that I am better attuned at what a photographer can say. I appreciate the particular angle from which an image can be shot or how a scene can be composed in a certain manner. I suspect that people who paint, cook, or play a musical instrument can also appreciate better another's creative work by having expertise in the craft itself.

The Protective Benefits of Art

There is now considerable evidence that both creating art and appreciating it can help prevent or at least lessen the blow of mental illness. In one study, a large cohort of healthy older adults without any signs of dementia were asked about their leisure activities and how often they engaged in them. When these individuals were followed-up five years later, those that had indicated dancing or playing a musical instrument as part of their leisure activities were less likely to develop dementia (also playing board games and reading were advantageous). In fact, playing a musical instrument throughout one's life—both early on and later in life—offers potent benefits in maintaining cognitive functions in many domains, including working memory and verbal recall.

When we get artistic we use our brain fully. The interlacing of sensations, thoughts, and feelings when we create and behold art helps us maintain existing neural pathways and create new ones (remember the neuroscientist's adage—*neurons that fire together, wire together*). Even beyond the benefits of physical activity, thinking and acting creatively, such as when we paint, play music, or dance, keeps the brain and body fully engaged. Importantly, when we express ourselves creatively we garner a sense of satisfaction that boosts self-esteem and reduces stress. It is this emotional lift that helps protect us against anxiety and depression.

Acquiring an artistic skill, such as playing the piano or ballroom dancing, is much like a sports skill. We start with repetitive learning of movements, usually with feedback from an instructor, and develop a proficiency in performance. After years of practice the skill becomes habitual or what psychologists call a procedural skill. Procedural skills require sensorimotor coordination and are quite different from the way the brain retains conceptual knowledge or personal memories. Most importantly, procedural skills can be expressed without the medial temporal lobe, which is so important for fact learning and remembering the past. That's why many call skill learning "muscle memory," because once we learn a skill we don't have to "retrieve" the memory of it, we just let our muscles perform the task. Of course, procedural skill memory is in your brain not in your muscles. Yet such skills are stored differently in your brain than fact knowledge or personal memories. Indeed, procedural skills (e.g., playing the piano), can be fairly well intact in patients with Alzheimer's disease, as such skills are stored in brain areas not affected by the disease.

A case in point is Willem deKooning, the 20th century abstract painter who exhibited memory decline during the 1980s and was ultimately diagnosed with Alzheimer's disease. His paintings during this period display a fluent, graceful style that is different from yet reminiscent of his earlier works. Critics do not agree as to the significance of these later works, which were likely created in the shadows of severe cortical deterioration. I, however, find them interesting and rather stunning displays of artistry, despite his mental disorder. Near the end of the decade, as the disease progressed, he was stripped of many mental functions, including art knowledge, planning, and organization, and his final works at the end of the 1980s seem to reflect this condition.

Regardless of one's capabilities, making art can be fun and therapeutic. Since 1988, local chapters of the Alzheimer's Association have sponsored *Memories in the Making*, a community program in which patients learn to express themselves through painting. In these programs, patients meet with artists who generously offer their assistance to help turn memories and feelings into artistic creations. As loss of cognitive function often leaves the Alzheimer patient isolated and emotionally restrained, expression through art offers a means of communicating to family and friends, particularly when language abilities falter. The artworks created also act as reminders for the patients of past experiences and memories.

When we behold someone else's artwork, we empathize with the artist and conjure up a story told metaphorically through visuals, sounds, or movements. Such creative sensations activate a myriad of brain systems as we tend to engage ourselves fully with those works of art that excite us. In concert with the gerontologist's adage of *use it or lose it*, the beholding of art protects us from mental dystrophy by activating broad neural circuits that form paths between sensations, memories, and feelings.

The therapeutic benefit of experiencing art has been promoted by many museums and community organizations. For example, the *ARTZ* program offered by the *I'm Still Here Foundation* encourages patients with Alzheimer's disease to experience art through organized group visits to various art museums, including the *Museum of Modern Art, Harvard Art Museum, Crocker Art Museum* and even the *Louvre* in Paris. *ARTZ* also organizes group outings to movies, science museums and other cultural events. Such outings act as cognitive stimulants, improve self-esteem, and offer an opportunity for social engagement.

Express Yourself!

Given what we know about creativity and artistic expression, here are some basic guidelines: 1) be knowledgeable—take lessons and learn about the history of your craft, 2) think divergently—let your mind go wild, brainstorm, and avoid filtering or screening out possibilities, 3) imagine globally—think of the big picture, consider broad goals and intentions, 4) work with metaphors—try linking remote associations through visual analogies, 5) produce a product—it may not be earth-shattering but it will be your own creation. It is the act of getting artistic that is important and as much a physical act as a mental one.

Our art becomes a part of ourselves as they are the embodiment of personal thoughts and feelings. In my own fun with photography, I find that my favorite shots are ones that render a feeling or tell a personal story that others can identify. There is a sense of ego-gratification when someone else enjoys or appreciates your art. However, it is best to consider that facet as an added bonus with the act of creating being the primary goal. Thus, you don't necessarily have to show your work to others. The main goal is the creative act, and we can all work to hone our craft. So get out the paints, camera equipment, dancing shoes, mixing bowls, guitar, or whatever you need for your creations and get artistic.

We can be artistic even when we don't have on our painter's beret or dancing shoes. Whenever we think in a novel way that fully activates our sensations, thoughts, and feelings we engage ourselves creatively. We may solve a problem in a new way or notice something on TV or the internet that stimulates our creative juices. The goal is to activate our brains fully and in a way that is different from what is familiar to us. You should be encouraged to watch a movie, see a musical performance, go to the theatre, or visit an art gallery and consider how an artwork or performance makes you think of the world or yourself in new ways. Importantly, when you leave the house and engage with others to get artistic you also get social and moving at the same time!

Get Artistic!

Be Creative!	Whip up something new — a song, poem, painting, recipe.
Be Imaginative	Think in terms of analogies and metaphors — link up different thoughts.
Old Tricks	Dust off that old instrument, camera, paint box, or cookbook.
Learn From Art	Go to the art museum, theater, movies, concert and talk about it.
New Stuff	Learn a new artistic skills: take a class or watch video tutorials.

Chapter 5: Get Responsive!

Your brain was not meant to be hanging around the house in front of a TV, computer, or newspaper. You have gathered knowledge from these and other sources for a purpose, which is to interact and respond efficiently with the world around you. When you get social, moving, and artistic you are forced to respond and share the knowledge stored in that 3-pound slab of tissue above your shoulders. It's time now to *get responsive* in every aspect of daily living. Action and reaction—it is not just a physical law, it should be your mental mantra from now on.

Your Responsive Brain

For many years, memory researchers were mostly concerned with the "learning" process or how we get information into our brains. They were less concerned with the retrieval process, or how we get information out. It is now evident that our memories are strengthened tremendously by retrieving them. Plato initiated our traditional view of the learning process when he likened memory to making impressions onto a ball of wax, which was the way ancient Greeks sealed and authenticated messages. As he described in *Theaetetus*: "I would have you imagine, then, that there exists in the mind of man a block of wax...when we wish to remember anything which we have seen, or heard, or thought in our own minds, we hold the wax to the perceptions and thoughts, and in that material receive the impression of them as from the seal of a ring."

Plato's view of learning conforms to what psychologists call a "bottom-up" process. The *bottom-up* notion refers to perceptions that "move up" to create knowledge. This idea is commensurate with Plato's sealing wax metaphor as knowledge is viewed as impressions made by perceptions. However, we now regard this one-way path to knowledge as entirely inefficient. Long-lasting memories depend on a constant interplay between bottom-up *and* top-down processes. Top-down processes refer to the way prior knowledge can guide (move down) and determine which perceptions are relevant. Social conversation is a good example of using top-down processing. In order to communicate efficiently it is best to use your knowledge to guide the course of a conversation. If someone asks, "Did you like the new restaurant?" it would be useful to know the likes and dislikes of the person who asked the question.

We apply top-down processing to build long-lasting memories. There is so much information in the world that we need to select and focus on relevant perceptions. Also, the more you know, the easier it is to build on that knowledge. Consider what you've learned in your job or even from a favorite pastime or hobby. Think how hard it would be to tell someone with no knowledge at all what you've learned—that is, starting with a blank block of wax. I once had the unenviable task of explaining baseball to a foreigner who knew nothing about the game (I was also on the other side of this knowledge gap when I turned on the TV in London and tried to understand what was going on in a cricket match). The more one knows about a topic, the easier it is to gain new information. There is interplay between bottom-up and top-down processes. In all of our learning experiences there is this "action-reaction" dynamics. Thus, learning is not just stamping new impressions into our brains—we need to use what we already know to gain most efficiently from new experiences.

How can we enhance top-down processing? Well, it is our old friend the prefrontal cortex that allows us to monitor and guide our attention. When we are "paying attention" we are mindful of what we are experiencing and can better relate the new with the old. Thus, whenever you encounter an interesting piece of information, respond to it by asking yourself: "How does this new piece of information fit in with what I already know?" "How is it useful?" The critical point here is to make a new fact meaningful to you. Thus, the more we think about a new experience and how it is related to what we already know, the better integrated that new information will be with existing knowledge.

It turns out that there is an incredibly easy way to enhance top-down processing—it is called the *generation effect* and should be practiced daily. In its simplest form you just repeat aloud what you've just learned. For example, a common complaint among older adults is the failure to remember the name of someone you just met. To apply the generation effect simply say the person's name out loud, such as responding, "Hello Mary, pleased to meet you." By generating the name, you've paid attention to it and just as importantly you've made sure that you got the name correct in the first place. Psychologists have shown that the generation effect can boost your memory by 30-50%, without much effort at all.

In my laboratory we measured brain activity while individuals generated information. We had individuals read word pairs, such as QUARREL-FIGHT or generated the second word from a fragment, GARBAGE-W_ST_. When individuals had to generate the second word (e.g., WASTE), a broad neural circuit was activated which included the prefrontal cortex and regions in the back of the brain known to be involved in thinking and imagining. Across all subjects, generated words were remembered 34% better than read words. Interestingly, memory performance could be predicted by the degree to which this "generation" neural circuit was active during learning. Thus, by generating information during learning (e.g., "Glad to meet you, Mary"), your brain will be more active and you'll remember the information better.

The generation effect is related to a set of mnemonic techniques known as *retrieval practice*. In my role as a university professor, students often complained that they had read a textbook chapter several times and still couldn't remember the information. This sentiment has some validity as research has shown that merely re-reading material does little to increase long-term memory for conceptual information. Long-lasting retention is significantly improved when students close their book after reading a chapter and try to retrieve what they've just read. The more you can restate in your own words what you've learned, the better you will remember the information later on. Also, after trying to retrieve information you know immediately what you cannot remember, and thus you can go back to the book chapter and re-study specific parts. In my view, retrieval practice—that is, testing yourself repeatedly—is one of the essential keys to efficient student learning.

Outside the classroom, there are important benefits to retrieval practice, particularly as we grow older. Sadly, the brain circuit involved in the generation effect is the very same network that is damaged by Alzheimer's disease. You won't necessarily prevent Alzheimer's disease by engaging in such mnemonic techniques, but such practices will keep active those very brain regions affected.

Retrieval practice forces you to respond to what you've learned. Consciously make an effort to think about how new information is related to other things that you know (e.g., top-down processing). You can engage in this mnemonic technique on a daily basis. Whenever you come across an interesting piece of information—from the news, internet, or a conversation, simply tell someone what you've just learned and that information will be stored more strongly in your brain. It is exceedingly simple to initiate this routine, and it will increase your retention tremendously. It also encourages you to get social by regularly conversing with others and telling them what you have recently learned.

"When One Teaches Two Learn"

This quote, by the noted science fiction author Robert A. Heinlein, points to what educators know very well—that teaching is the best way to learn. For one thing, it demands retrieval practice, as instructors must reiterate what they have learned. Yet effective teaching is more than just spouting out knowledge as one needs to present information in a way that is meaningful to the student and encourages learning. Just as an architect must design a structure before it is built, effective teaching requires the planning and organizing of material with the end product being the construction of an engaging presentation. Through this process, teaching not only helps the student learn, but it also strengthens the teacher's knowledge. By delving into the mechanics of effective teaching, we gain insight into the way the brain itself learns and retains knowledge.

One way to characterize the knowledge stored in your brain is to think of it as a vast web of connected information—your personal *Wikipedia*.

Gaining new knowledge is thus a matter of linking new information with what you already know. By this view, effective teaching not only requires a presentation of relevant facts but more importantly a way of connecting the facts to the student's existing knowledge base. It is thus critical to have a preconceived idea of how a topic is organized (i.e., how the facts are connected) and to present at the outset a barebones version of that organization. This overview gives the student some knowledge before getting into the details. If an instructor fails to provide an outline of material at the outset, students can become confused as it is difficult to see how facts are related.

Psychologists use the term *schema* to describe the skeletal framework or outline of a topic. For example, the schema of this book is structured around the five steps for a healthy brain with the acronym *SMART* to help you remember them. Under each step are three or four subtopics delineated by chapter headings, such as the current heading—*"When One Teaches Two Learn."* Facts presented in this book can then be organized with respect to each *Get SMART* step and the headings within each chapter. In Chapter 1, I suggested that you read the headings prior to delving into a chapter. This suggestion was my way of encouraging you to develop a schema for each chapter before getting into the details.

When learning is viewed as linking new information to existing knowledge, it becomes essential to consider what the learner *already knows*. Many instructors fail because they assume too much existing knowledge and present material to students as if they were experts in the field. On the other hand, if one assumes that students know absolutely nothing they fall prey to talking down to them and boring them to death. The problem with teaching to large groups is that students will undoubtedly have different background levels of knowledge. There are, however useful tips that will draw all learners into a new topic. First, as mentioned earlier with respect to creative thinking (Chapter 4), make ample use of metaphors and analogies. They work by connecting new information with what is already known. For example, by characterizing knowledge as your personal *Wikipedia*, one gains a sense of the interconnectedness of knowledge and how new information can be added by creating new links to existing knowledge. Likewise, by comparing a teacher to an architect, one begins to appreciate the importance of planning and organizing before construction. We have general knowledge of how *Wikipedia* and architects work, and such knowledge can be useful in helping to characterize new concepts.

Another way to link new information with existing knowledge is by infusing the learning session with examples from everyday experiences. In teaching parlance, it basically means to *make it meaningful*. I believe that any topic can and should be related to everyday experiences, and the more the instructor can link what is to be presented to real world knowledge, the better it will be understood and retained. It is useful to begin a learning session with an everyday situation, as it sets up a schema before one gets going with the details. Plato's analogy of memory as an impression onto sealing wax was his way of characterizing learning with an everyday experience (at least one in the life of 4th Century BC Greeks). All good teachers infuse their lectures with metaphors, analogies, and everyday examples to anchor new information to the student's existing knowledge base.

Perhaps the most difficult aspect of teaching is to keep students interested and motivated throughout a course and during each lecture. We can all remember those extraordinary teachers whose lectures were thoughtful, engaging, and full of interesting material. We also can remember those days when going to a lecture felt like a near-death experience (only without the light at the end of the tunnel). Whether we like it or not good teachers are those that can entertain. By making learning enjoyable and interesting, students become active participants in their learning experience. Instructors don't have to be stand-up comics (though it wouldn't hurt), but they do have to engage students during class and keep them interested.

How can one make learning fun? Most people enjoy reading a news item, listening to a radio program, watching a documentary film, or going to a museum. These activities are entertaining as we learn through *stories* that capture our interest and emotions.

When I say "stories," I'm referring to presentations that begin with a premise, engage the listener with issues that have interesting turns, and then end by tying facts and details together. We associate this format with fictional dramas, though it should be considered when teaching facts and concepts. Indeed, early storytelling, such the telling of those epic Homeric tales, the *Odyssey* and *Iliad*, were intended as much to inform as to entertain. To make any material engaging we should try to tell stories rather than lecture. Many students enjoy watching and learning from informational videos on the internet, such as the popular TED talks. These presentations are limited to 18 minutes, which is enough time for the speaker to present a topic in some detail but not too long to exceed one's attention span. Also, the presenters have been vetted in advance to be interesting and engaging speakers. Although humor is definitely a feature in maintaining interest, a key aspect is the way the speaker tells a story.

The *Exploratorium* in San Francisco is one of the premier science museums in the world. It offers visitors a panoply of wonderfully hands-on exhibits. There are few occasions that can provide a more fun and engaging learning experience than a trip to a museum. The founder of the *Exploratorium*, Frank Oppenheimer, understood the advantages of this setting, especially when compared to the stigma of classroom learning. He said, "No one ever flunks a museum." Why shouldn't all of our learning experiences be fun and engaging? It's a bit harder in a classroom, but the more learning can be done by active participation, the better. In my psychology courses, I have tried to involve the students with demonstrations of experiments. Educators recommend dividing a class into small groups (3 to 4 students) for a set time period (5-10 minutes) and having groups consider a problem or controversy. Students often dislike such tasks, perhaps because it actually forces them to participate and discuss issues. Yet any time one engages in active participation, learning improves.

Given our recent understanding of the benefits of retrieval practice, I believe that a dramatic change in the standard practice of college teaching is forthcoming. No longer should an instructor stand up and pontificate for an hour, which far exceeds the attention span of the typical college student. Instead, a lecture should be divided into three 10-12 minute mini-lectures or sections each presenting an encapsulated issue—a short story (or chapter of a longer story). At the end of each section students should engage in active retrieval practice—they should be tested on their knowledge of the just presented material. The instructor could formulate thought questions and have students answer them individually or put them in groups for discussion. A key factor is to encourage students to conceptualize material for themselves. Such retrieval practice exercises create an active learning environment, which will dramatically improve learning and retention.

These various teaching tips—from presenting a schema to retrieval practice—encourage the learner to engage in top-down processing or what educators call *active learning*. It is the learner who must participate by determining how new information is to be incorporated into their personal knowledge base. Good teaching facilitates active learning by providing a framework before presenting details, making information meaningful through metaphors and everyday examples, and telling engaging stories that inform. Importantly, the act of teaching in this manner forces the instructor to engage in his or her own active learning process and thus create a well-integrated, long-lasting knowledge base. There are programs—both nationally and locally—that offer teaching opportunities. In Chapter 2, I mentioned taking course offered by the *Osher Lifelong Learning Institute*. These courses are taught by volunteers who have an interest in telling their stories. It is possible to offer your services as an instructor through this program or other local programs at community centers, colleges, senior centers, or public libraries.

Even if you have no plans to engage in formal teaching, you should always keep these tips in mind whenever you are learning a new concept or reading about a new area of interest. Be sure you construct a schema by formulating a working outline of the material, *before you get into the details*. Think about how new information is related to everyday experiences and try to link concepts with existing knowledge. Finally, practice retrieving the information by telling anyone who is willing to listen what you have learned. Work on these teaching tips on a daily basis whenever you encounter new knowledge.

Tell the World How You Feel

When you get emotional you also get responsive. Emotions motivate us to "do something about it." You might think that it is the overly optimistic, "la di da" kind of person who lives the longest, because they appear to not have a care in the world. In truth, that personality trait is not as destined for old age compared to the somewhat pessimistic—some might say grumpy—individual. Overly optimistic people are less worried about their health and tend to participate in risky activities. Individuals who are concerned about themselves and the world around them are more willing to do something about the situation. Indeed, conscientiousness is the personality disposition that is most strongly related to longevity.

If something bothers you, *respond* to your feelings. Get involved with things that concern you. You can become active in a variety of ways by being involved in community affairs, volunteering your services, helping those less fortunate than you, or simply writing to your congressperson. By acting upon your feelings, you get socially involved, physically active, and creative. As mentioned earlier, volunteering is one of the best ways to keep a healthy brain as you apply your talents (or at least your body) to assist others. My feeling is that it is not just being grumpy or complaining that is related to longevity. Rather, it is the ability to turn complaints into actions that is key. Conscientious individuals not only live longer, they are actually happier and have a stronger sense of self worth. So go ahead and get annoyed, but do something about it.

Another way to put feelings to work is keep in mind what I call the "aesthetic query." That is, whenever you come across something new—a new product, movie, book, song—ask yourself, "Do I like it?" "Does it interest me?" "Why or why not?" When we ask such questions we *get responsive* in an emotional way and impart some value to an item (from like very much to dislike very much). Moreover, when we consider why we like something (or not), we have to think and evaluate the item to justify our emotions. Critics—of movies, books, art, and music—must address such issues in their professional lives. We regard their views because we know that worthy evaluations require vast knowledge and expertise in the field. These days when I speak to educators about ways to improve student learning, I encourage them to have students consider the aesthetics questions. Rather than merely going over some recently learned material, such as a novel, ask students if they liked the book, if it was interesting, and why or why not. By simply asking, "Do you like it?" students get personally involved and become mindful of their response. Also, there really is no right or wrong answer to the question, as it's merely a matter of opinion.

You might enjoy novels, movies, food, wine, or music. You might enjoy new products, such as the newest digital gadget or rage in fashion. Whatever it is that you like, become your own critic and ask yourself, "Why do I like it?" Addressing aesthetic questions requires you to justify your response. Moreover, the more you learn about movies, fashion, or music, the better you'll be at evaluating new products. For instance, you might enjoy drinking wine. With education and practice(!), you can begin to appreciate how various grapes and regions produce different taste sensations. By getting emotionally involved and evaluating why you like something, you enjoy yourself and become educated at the same time. You don't necessarily have to make your evaluations public—though of course you should be encouraged to tell people what you like (or dislike) for the purpose of retrieval practice. These days it is easy to join or even start a book club or similar "critics' corner where friends meet for group discussions.

Another way to express your feelings is to create a "web log," which was the original term for what we now call a *blog*. Blogs have in many ways replaced magazine and newspaper articles as many web-centric individuals get their daily news and fun facts through blogs. Your blog can pertain to anything that interests you, from information about hobbies to random thoughts about the world. If you like to travel, create a blog of your trips with tips on things to do, photos, and links to favorite places you've visited. Such a travel blog gives you a permanent scrapbook of your excursions. The best blogs are those that read like magazine articles or editorials—well written relatively short entries ranging from 300 to 600 words. There are free sites that allow you to create your own blog, which after some fairly easy instruction is not any more difficult than writing with a word processor.

Some view blogging as something "young kids" do who aspire to become accomplished journalists. Indeed, creative bloggers can attract quite a following, which can lead to some fame. I encourage you, however, to blog with the sole intent of getting yourself responsive and expressing yourself through creative writing (or even non-creative writing!). The important point is to write for yourself as a way of organizing your thoughts. You may have always wanted to be a food or movie critic and through blog posts you can talk about your favorite restaurants or movies. Perhaps you found a new recipe and came up with a new dish to include your cooking repertoire— write about it! Blogging forces you to react to your environment and respond to recent experiences. As with teaching, this very act will strengthen your own memories. Moreover, if you do forget a recipe, restaurant, movie, or travel experience, you can refer back to your own blog entries!

Just Do It!

To get responsive, you need to apply yourself on a daily basis. Talk about it, write about it, act upon it...just do it and you'll build stronger memories. Aging researchers advocate the importance of engaging yourself as you learn. You might recall that in Chapter 1, I mentioned the study of nuns who were evaluated on a regular basis across their life span. In one analysis, autobiographies written by these nuns just prior to formal entry into the congregation were evaluated. The sophistication of these early writings (e.g., number of ideas packed into a sentence) was related to better preserved cognitive abilities in old age as well as reduced Alzheimer's pathology in their brains after death. One implication of this study is that those who worked on writing skills and could generate well formed text at an early age were better protected from Alzheimer's disease later in life. The practice of writing is one of the best ways to organize one's thoughts and get responsive.

I recommend that throughout your life you write things down. One simple thing that I do to help me remember personal events is to write a brief description of things that happened to me at the end of each day (or the next morning if I forget!). This daily log is not meant to be a "dear diary" of deep seated feelings, but rather a listing of events. I may write down what I did for exercise, what movie I watched, or who I saw that day. I use a spreadsheet with the date written in the first column and a one sentence description of the day's events in the next column. The mere act of writing it down strengthens my memory, and if I do forget, I have a written chronicle of my (rather mundane) life.

Our hobbies are constructive ways to get responsive. You may enjoy gardening, carpentry, cooking, photography, or fixing things. Just do it! As mentioned, if you're skilled at any of these or other creative endeavors, consider teaching or tutoring. On a daily basis, take information in, relate new experiences with what you already know, and tell someone else what you've learned. If you're going to watch TV, tell someone about the great shows you've seen. Get responsive and engage yourself with the world.

Get Responsive!

Say It!	Practice retrieval by telling others what you've learned.
Use it!	Start a club, work on your hobby, react to the world around you.
Teach It!	Teach a course or tutor at a local school, library, or community center.
Evaluate it!	Ask the aesthetic question: Why do I like (or don't like) it?
Blog It!	Write it down, share experiences, be a critic, keep a daily log of events.

Chapter 6: Get Thinking!

When you picked up this book, you may have thought that the first step toward a healthy brain was to *get thinking*. You should realize by now that *all* of the prior steps are meant to engage your thinking brain *and more*. Also, if I had started with *get thinking* and reversed the order I'd have to call this book, *Get TRAMS*, and include a bunch of train puns. But let's not get off track and consider specific routines that can optimize your thinking abilities.

Thinking About the Brain

"Neurons that fire together, wire together." I mentioned this saying in Chapter 1 and if you keep it in mind, it will remind you of the importance of encouraging organized brain activity. When you *get thinking*, you stimulate your brain in a coordinated manner, and the best way to do this is to *get social, moving, artistic,* and *responsive.* These activities wire your brain as a unit making it more efficient and better integrated. Being mentally alert is the result of coordinated brain circuits, and it is the prefrontal cortex that helps us direct and control brain activity. We are always bombarded by multiple thoughts and possible actions, which is fine, but at some point we need to focus on one particular idea or response. The prefrontal cortex monitors and guides your thoughts, allowing you to sharpen your attention, screen out stray ideas, and implement appropriate actions.

Psychologists use the term *metacognition* (i. e., "above" cognition) to refer to your ability to supervise mental processes and apply strategies for organized thinking. Tom Nelson, an early metacognitive researcher and graduate school mentor of mine, developed a model that describes metacognition as the interplay between "object-level" and "meta-level" processes. Object-level processes are the numerous cognitive functions that enable us to interact with the world, such as being aware of where you are, what you're doing, and with whom you are conversing. These processes are controlled by a "meta-level" that *monitors* these object-level processes and then controls their activity. For example, you may be trying to chat with a friend at a party in the midst of distracting noise. Through metacognitive monitoring and control, you are able to suppress stray conversations and focus on what your friend is saying (or if you prefer move your attention to the juicier conversation next to you).

The meta-level directs your thoughts and guides your actions toward the specific task at hand. Nelson's model of metacognition offers a way of describing how the prefrontal cortex implements executive control. The prefrontal cortex is your supervisory meta-level which monitors what's going on in the back of your brain where object-level processes reside. Actually there doesn't seem to be a single supervisor or "brain CEO," but rather a board of supervisors, each one controlling a particular mental process, such seeing, hearing, feeling or moving. By this view, the prefrontal cortex includes several executive controllers each adjusting brain activity occurring in the posterior cortex. In this way, we have a flexible brain that allows you to think more efficiently and adjust to changing task demands.

When it comes to aging, our brains go through multiple changes. As mentioned in Chapter 1, an overall slowing of brain processing is common, which is reflected in being a little more scattered in thought and having a harder time retrieving information, such as words being on "the tip of your tongue." On top of this generalized slowing we incur a disproportionate amount of cortical shrinkage in the prefrontal cortex. Imagine your poor metacognitive supervisor dealing with rather slow employees, and we begin to understand better those annoying occurrences of failing to remember a friend's name, a doctor's appointment, or where you put your keys.

There are simple ways to work around many of these senior moments. One easy solution is to *write things down* on a notepad or on your smartphone. Make a to-do list or entry in a daily calendar (electronic or otherwise). I actually have a particular ailment that I call *car amnesia*, which occurs sometimes when I return to a large parking lot, such as at an airport or sports event. It results in confusion and frustration and often excessive walking around in circles. These days to avoid car amnesia, I take a photo of my car with my smartphone as I leave the lot.

This act focuses my attention on the car's location and provides a visual cue upon my return (of course, I still have to remember to do this before I leave the lot!). In the case of forgetting where you put your glasses or keys, my solution is to *always* set them down in the same location. In your home find a spot—a hook by your door, a corner on your bedside table—and put your keys and glasses on the same spot *every time*.

In addition to these physical reminders, research has shown that high-functioning individuals can develop brain responses that compensate for deficits due to aging. In one study, individuals read or listened to words and were asked to commit these items to memory. Following this study phase, they were placed in an fMRI scanner and asked not just to remember the words but also to recall if they had been previously studied as a read or heard item. This kind of "source memory" draws heavily on the prefrontal cortex, particularly the right prefrontal cortex, as it involves focused attention and directed memory retrieval. Interestingly, older adults who performed well on the test not only showed greater activity in the right prefrontal cortex, a finding that was expected, but they also showed heightened activity in the left prefrontal cortex, as if this brain region was additionally recruited as a compensatory response. Neither low-performing older adults or any of the young adults showed this additional brain activation.

High functioning individuals have the capacity to move mental resources around and compensate for the gradual changes associated with aging. The more brain reserve you have, the better able you'll be to adapt to changes. Imagine a small company that has only one skilled person for each task. If a worker gets sick, then it will be difficult to compensate for that person's duties, and the entire production will falter. If there are reserves of workers trained to perform multiple tasks, then production can proceed without much disruption. Similarly, some people's brains—through better genes and a healthier lifestyle—are better able to multi-task so that a brain region not typically used for a particular task may be recruited when another region falters. The greater the capacity of your brain to find flexible alternatives, the better able you'll be to prevent those nagging senior moments.

Evidence for "cognitive reserve" in high functioning brains has been observed in studies of individuals with Alzheimer's disease. In the course of the disease many brain regions become affected. Yet highly educated, successful individuals are better able to compensate for cognitive declines during the early stages of the disease. The consequence of having such cognitive reserve is that successful brains can stave off incipient declines even though they are being ravaged by Alzheimer brain pathology. In fact, if you compare the brain of a highly educated individual who has just been diagnosed with Alzheimer's disease with the brain of a less educated individual at the same stage of mental status, the brain of the highly educated individual will actually be in a more advanced stage of pathology and they will die sooner from the disease. This fact suggests that high functioning individuals can use their cognitive reserve and hold off mental declines. Ultimately when the reserves are used up, declines appear, though much later in the disease state.

Flexibility is the key to a healthy brain. Find different ways to activate your mind and restructure your brain with alternate ways of doing things. Extending one's domain and moving away from the routinized activities engages the prefrontal cortex and metacognitive processes because novel or alternate methods require focused attention—that is, the monitoring and control of thought processes. Build up that cognitive reserve by developing new tools and resources for future applications.

Are Brain Games Worth It?

Much news and controversy have arisen over *brain games*—those commercially available computer programs marketed to increase brain fitness and stave off Azheimer's disease. Prior to their advancement, many advocated traditional "brain games," such as card playing, crossword puzzles, and Sudoku as ways to exercise your brain. Are these activities worth it? Can regular involvement with video games improve your attention and memory? Even better, will they protect you from future mental declines or even brain disease?

Some argue that the computer revolution has made us dumber as we have become more dependent on memory "prosthetic" devices (e. g., smartphones, computers). Who needs to memorize phone numbers, addresses, birthdays, road directions and other items that in the past had to be committed to memory. At the touch of our fingertips we can access a vast array of knowledge so efficiently that those arguments about who sang what song or starred in what movie can be resolved within seconds. Has technology corrupted our brains? Are we not exercising our memories enough? It is my feeling that if anything we have become smarter and mentally more facile with the advent of computer technology. Having knowledge at our fingertips allows us to use that information more directly and apply it to think more creatively. Moreover, we can appear more socially responsible by being able to remember someone's birthday or even better one's wedding anniversary!

Brain games are meant to be entertaining yet geared to engage mental abilities known to decline with aging. As such, they are based on psychological tests of attention, multi-tasking, and memory, yet are presented in a fun game-like environment. For example, you may be asked to control a racing car, speed boat, or other fast moving vehicle while trying to avoid obstacles. You may be asked to remember a sequence of colorful shapes or recall where those shapes were located on the screen before they disappeared. These programs monitor your level of performance and adjust to your personal abilities so they can be demanding yet not exceedingly difficult. You begin at a suitable level and are then pushed a bit above this comfort level on a day by day schedule. With regular practice, you'll see significant improvement in your scores on these mental games.

Most brain games focus on *cognitive control* processes as these functions engage the prefrontal cortex and, as we have discussed, it is this brain region that is most affected in aging. In everyday activities we engage our prefrontal when we need to apply mental control, such as backing the car out of a parking spot or deciding how best to plan daily events. When we apply cognitive control we are better able to entertain multiple thoughts in mind, block out irrelevant ones, and act accordingly. Without the prefrontal cortex thoughts are jumbled, confused and indecisive.

Not unlike a physical exercise program, brain games act as your personal trainer by taking you through daily mental calisthenics. If you like arcade games, crossword puzzles, or solitaire, you'll likely find brain games stimulating and enjoyable. Brain game developers contend that not only will you improve your level of performance on these specific games, you'll also improve mental efficiency in many other domains of daily living. Psychologists call this *transfer of learning*, and it is this issue that is the crux of the controversy over brain games. Will a commitment to brain games translate into overall cognitive improvement? Will you be more efficient at avoiding accidents while driving? Will you be less forgetful when you look for your keys or try to remember a person's name?

The findings have been mixed as to the benefits of brain games to overall proficiency in cognitive capacity. On the plus side, there are findings that demonstrate improved mental function following cognitive training in neurological patients with substantial cognitive impairment. In these cases, cognitive rehabilitation is geared toward facilitating the specific mental function impaired following a brain injury. Just as physical therapy can improve walking after a broken hip, cognitive therapy intended toward a specific mental disability, such as speech comprehension, can facilitate recovery of that function. Thus following neurological injury, such as a stroke or head trauma, mental exercises geared toward improving specific cognitive deficits can help.

What about the benefits of brain games for the average Joe or Jane who generally function well in daily life except perhaps for those nagging senior moments? Can we sharpen our brains in a general manner? It is this scientific point that is essential in addressing the benefits of brain games, yet it is the most difficult to answer. Most scientists maintain a guarded skepticism about the benefits of brain games, as many feel that claims by marketers have been exaggerated. In 2014, an international group of 70 cognitive scientists and neuroscientists signed a letter posted on the Stanford Center on Longevity website which stated: *"...at this point it is not appropriate to conclude that training-induced changes go significantly beyond the learned skills, that they affect broad abilities with real world relevance.* They go on to say that *"No studies have demonstrated that playing brain games cures or prevents Alzheimer's disease or other forms of dementia."* This point was reinforced by a careful analysis by psychologists who reviewed 132 published papers and found '*...little evidence that training enhances performance on distantly related tasks or that training improves everyday cognitive performance.* To make matters worse, the marketers of *Luminosity*, one of the better known brain training programs, agreed to pay $2 million after being charged by the Federal Trade Commission that the developers over-exaggerated their claims that playing their brain games will prevent memory loss and Alzheimer's disease.

Current investigations concerning the benefits of brain games have become more sophisticated. One of the leaders in the field, Adam Gazzaley from the University of California, San Francisco, is an expert in brain imaging and cognitive aging. Gazzaley's research has focused on trying to optimize brain games. The games that he has developed are geared toward cognitive control in speeded visual-spatial tasks. In "NeuroRacer" you must guide a fast moving car while making rapid decisions about targets along the road. Some targets require a response (hitting a button) while others are to be ignored. In his games, Gazzeley incorporates many features of frontal lobe function, such as selective attention, multi-tasking, interference control, and response inhibition. His findings and those from other laboratories have shown that brain game training can result in neural changes observable in functional neuroimaging. For example, after training enhanced brain activity in the frontal cortex has been found as measured by electroencephalography (EEG).

The major hurdle confronting the full-scale adoption of brain games is still the degree to which transfer occurs between daily video game exercises and improvements in everyday mental activities. One difficulty is the ability to assess actual benefits in mental sharpness. If one claims improvements merely on a subjective feeling of being "more alert," such sentiments can also be caused by the "placebo" effect of simply wanting to feel better because so much effort has been placed toward daily mental calisthenics. A better measure would be the number of mental "accidents" that occur (e.g., forgetting to take pills or remembering a doctor's appointment), yet such tallies are difficult to record, not all that frequent, and subject to forgetting to record mental mishaps.

Another concern is that most brain games focus specifically on frontal lobe functions, such as selective attention, multi-tasking, and inference control. Although it is true that such functions are the first to show age-related declines, it is also important to keep in mind that the prefrontal cortex does not do anything by itself. As described by our metacognition framework, the prefrontal cortex monitors and supervises activity in the rest of your thinking brain, and just as a conductor needs an accomplished set of musicians to produce beautiful music, your thought processes will not be up to snuff if other parts of your brain aren't working well. In order to think efficiently you'll need to engage your prefrontal cortex but also work on the specific "object-level" processes that are relevant to the task at hand. The question with respect to brain games is the extent to which pushing buttons while keeping track of objects on a video screen will actually coordinate your thought processes during everyday situations. Your "conductor" may be in great shape, but what about the rest of the orchestra?

So where do we stand? As with other enjoyable activities that stimulate your brain (e.g., card playing, crossword puzzles, Sudoku), brain games should be enjoyed for fun and entertainment. These pastimes will keep you mind active and exercise your brain. If, however, you don't particularly enjoy such activities and do so merely because you believe such mental calisthenics will transfer to other daily activities, you may be better off engaging in things that more closely resemble the kind of mental activities you enjoy or want to improve. Do you want to learn more from reading? Join a book club and discuss your thoughts with others. Do you want to be more attentive in daily activities? Practice the specific kinds of activities that demand such mental processes. Do you want to be creative? Learn a new musical piece, dance step, or dinner recipe. Explore new locations around your neighborhood. Go to a museum and think about how the exhibits tell a story—then tell others what you've learned. Do you want to be better able to remember things, such as your friends' names or places you've been? Spend time with your friends and reminisce about your past experiences. The bottom line (of course), is that you can dispense with brain games if you just *Get SMART*.

Be Mindful

Most of the time we exist in a rather mindless state. We walk, breath, chew gum, and even drive at great speeds without paying much attention to what we're doing. Our brains have become so familiar with our environment that we don't have to pay attention to routine occurrences, such as the changing appearance of objects as we walk around them or the way the sun casts shadows. Even as you read this sentence, you aren't aware of the squiggly marks that make up each word. Instead, you simply and automatically ascribe meaning to words. If this chapter were written in a completely unfamiliar language, you'd only see odd squiggly marks. In our overly regularized everyday world our brains simply take over, and we proceed without much thinking.

It is definitely a good thing that we can move about in a rather mindless fashion. I can remember the awkward anxiety during my high school driver's training class when I first sat behind the steering wheel. Every little action—pushing my foot down on the gas pedal, flipping the turn signal, turning the wheel—required conscious attention and effort. Now, of course, we all speed down the highway, maneuver around traffic, and chat with others without even thinking about it. Imagine if our experience of walking, reading, or driving was always like the first time we performed these actions. It would be mindboggling as every sensory stimulus, every motor movement would require attention. It is thus an immense advantage for us to be able to put a good deal of our everyday existence on autopilot.

When we do encounter something irregular, our brains take note, as it can be critically important to determine if an unexpected experience should cause us to be worried, excited, or fearful. Consider the situation—you walk up to your house after a trip to the store and find the front door ajar. You would of course notice this irregularity immediately and try to determine if you had accidently left the door open or if you should be worried about a break-in. The calm voice of your spouse chatting on the phone would readily set you at ease. Whenever we experience an unexpected change in the environment, neural signals are sent to your prefrontal cortex, which implore you to pay attention and *think* about what may have caused the break from the norm. In psychological terms, to be *mindful* is to focus your attention and become consciously aware of a perception (was the door forcibly opened?), a thought (did my spouse say he/she was coming home?), or a plan of action (what should I do now?). Mindful experiences engage the prefrontal cortex (i.e., executive control), thus allowing you to direct brain activity to relevant issues at hand (a perception, thought, or action).

What might be a rather unique human capacity—or at least something that we are really good at doing—is disregarding the physical world and spending a lot of brain power ruminating about the past or planning for the future. When we engage in such mental time travel—or even when we're just day dreaming—a set of brain regions are active which are collectively called the *default mode network*. This term is an unfortunate one and attributed to the serendipitous way it was discovered. As mentioned earlier, in a typical fMRI experiment, brain activity is compared between two time periods, such as times when your eyes are open compared to "rest" periods when your eyes are closed. In this way, scientists can cancel out extraneous brain activity unrelated to the task at hand and assess activity specifically involved in a particular mental function, such as vision.

A group of clever scientists, just out of curiosity, decided to assess the reverse comparison—that is, what part of the brain is active when you are resting instead of doing some activity. It turns out that a goodly amount of your cortex is active when you are in rest or "default" mode. Of course, our brains are never just sitting there doing "nothing." During these so-called rest periods, you are likely engaged in all sorts of mindful activities, such as preparing yourself for the next trial, thinking about what you've just done, or merely daydreaming. This "default mode" activity is best described as your *reflective thinking* mode. It is most active when you are reminiscing about the past, planning for the future, or simply mind wandering. This internal mindful state involves the prefrontal cortex because you are focusing attention on thoughts, memories, or plans.

Reflective thinking or rumination moves us internally. Alerting sounds or flashes of light will engage our prefrontal cortex and make us mindful of sensory signals. What about paying attention to familiar sensory experiences? That is, what if you spend time to *stop and smell the roses* (or at least the coffee). As our brains are geared to ignore the regularities of our everyday world, attending to such sensory regularities takes some practice. In Buddhist traditions, meditation training focuses on developing an awareness of sensory experiences. One meditative technique is the practice of paying attention to one's breathing. This highly routinized activity is almost always on autopilot, and thus it takes practice to focus your attention on the sensation. The trick is to focus your senses, such as feeling the pressure on your chest cavity as you breathe or the draft of air around your nostrils. What you don't do is *ruminate* about your breathing, such as telling yourself to inhale a certain amount or counting the number of times you breathe in. In fact, the point is to avoid engaging in reflective thoughts (default mode) and instead focus your attention on sensations.

Recently, scientists have become interested in sensory mindfulness. Rather than paying attention to your thoughts as you would in reflective thinking mode, you are asked to focus your attention on the here and now. You are basically telling your brain not to take your routine sensory world for granted—i.e., not go in autopilot mode—and pay attention to your sensory environment. What's fascinating about this Eastern-style meditative experience is that it activates brain circuits that are different from either the autopilot or reflective thinking modes. In particular, this so-called *salience mode*, activates the prefrontal cortex (which is not generally active in autopilot mode) and high-order sensory circuits (which is not generally active in reflective thinking mode).

The benefits of practicing sensory mindfulness are many, and Western clinicians and health programs are beginning to advocate meditative practices. Training oneself to pay attention to one's breathing has been used as a relaxation technique and extremely useful as a way to relieve stress and reduce insomnia. I have actually tried the attention-to-breathe method on those occasional sleepless moments around 3 am when I begin to ruminate over some stressful issue. It does seem to work, as my attention to sensations disengages me from the thoughts that are keeping me awake. It is difficult sometimes to concentrate on something that is so automatic, and it is easy to go astray and return to ruminating. I suspect further practice will increase my proficiency. Psychologists, such as Ellen Langer, are promoting sensory mindfulness practices, such as meditative training, as a way to encourage good mental health and successful aging.

Given the benefits of physical activity (*Get Moving!*) *and* meditative mindfulness (*Get Thinking!*), the neuroscientist Tracey Shors has advocated a dual activity exercise which she calls *Mental and Physical (MAP) Training*. Shors and colleagues conducted an experiment in which participants engaged in mindful meditation (attention to breathing) for 30 minutes immediately followed by 30 minutes of aerobic exercise (choreographed *Zumba* dancing). After eight weeks of MAP training, participants showed improvements in oxygen uptake and mental health (self-rated depression). These findings are preliminary in that it is not known whether the combination of meditative mindfulness and aerobic exercise actually produces any greater benefit than either two exercises in isolation. Also, it is not known whether such a regime would specifically benefit cognitive function such as attention or memory. However, given the established benefits of both mindfulness training and aerobic exercise, such dual-activity regimes offer a way to integrate both physical and mental exercise in a single daily routine.

Make it New!

How can we *get thinking*? A simple way is to *make it new*. Our brains are geared to pay particular attention to novel events. Evolutionarily speaking, it is essential to focus on unfamiliar situations, as it's through new experiences that we learn about a changing environment. Imagine an early hominid foraging through the woods and encountering a never-before-seen fruit. The consequences of eating that fruit could significantly determine whether that individual survives or not, as the fruit could provide nourishment or cause sickness. Our brains go into heightened awareness when we encounter new experiences. These days we can enrich our mental environment by co-opting this survival mechanism and work on seeking new experiences, new adventures, even in our rather mundane everyday existence.

Novelty engages our thinking brain by making experiences distinctive. Consider memory for a recent vacation trip. After such trips, we can recall numerous outings and events—what we did, where we ate, whom we saw. How well can you remember events during a particular work week from, say, two months ago? On vacation, every day is a distinct novel event and our entire brain—sensations, thoughts, and feelings—kicks in when we encounter such new experiences. You can imagine the prefrontal cortex becoming engaged on vacation as new and unfamiliar events demand attention as we enter a focused sensory (salience) mode. These new sensations generate thoughts and plans of action, thus engaging our reflective thinking mode, as well. Interestingly, the hippocampus, that brain structure so critical for episodic memory (see Chapter 1), is as much a "novelty detector" as it is a storage mechanism. That is, the hippocampus goes into overdrive during novel situations as if it is telling the rest of the brain to take note and commit these new experiences to memory. Of course, we don't have to spend exorbitant amounts of money for vacations. We can all experience novel events on a daily basis—vary your daily walking routine, explore new places around town, seek novelty!

Given our brain's desire for new experiences, we must explore and break away from familiar habits. To substantiate this notion, Denise Park and colleagues conducted a large psychological study in which 106 older adults (age 60-90 years) participated in a 14-week cognitive training program in which they were taught new skills. One group learned to use a digital camera and edit their shots using *Photoshop*, the computer program that enables users to adjust and enhance their images. Another group learned to quilt from a professional who also taught participants to use a computer-driven sewing machine. Other (control) participants took classes that involved more receptive activities (playing games, watching movies, cooking), which relied on existing knowledge rather than learning new skills. Participants spent 15 hours a week in class sessions, and at the end of the 3-month program all were given clinical tests of episodic memory. Significant enhancement of memory and new learning ability was shown in participants who engaged in novel skill training (photography, quilting) compared to those who participated in the more receptive activities.

Of the two engagement programs, the photography course was the more challenging and also produced the most benefit in episodic memory. The authors attribute the benefits of this course as a result of the rather difficult task of learning *Photoshop*. In a follow-up study, Park and colleagues focused on the benefits of learning new computer skills. Older adults (ages 60-90 years old) took a 10-week course on using an *iPad*. They spent 15 hours each week on instructions and exercises that involved ways to use the computer tablet, such as information access, social networking, health monitoring, and financial management. After the 10-week program, these individuals not only acquired new computer skills, but also their episodic memory was significantly improved compared to a control group who met each week and participated in more receptive interactions (playing games, social conversation).

Many older adults have difficulty acquiring computer-based skills as the technology wasn't available when they were young. There is often a daunting anxiety—almost fear—of anything that reeks with computer technology, even though these days most devices (e.g., tablets, smartphones) are fairly easy to use, when given initial tutoring. I encourage everyone to develop these skills as it can be incredibly useful—even life saving—to have information at your fingertips. Also, one can easily manage so many useful things, such as appointments, health status, and finances. With applications such as *Wikipedia* and *YouTube*, you can quickly access volumes of information and how-to videos. These days most public libraries offer electronic books (e-books) to borrow and read through on-line services such as *Overdrive.com*, thus providing free access to thousands of books that can be read on a tablet or even smartphone.

We should encourage novel experiences in our lives as often as possible. Visit *different* locales, try *unfamiliar* foods, strike up a conversation with *new* acquaintances. Stimulate your brain by making it new—everyday! Keep in mind that a healthy brain involves the engagement of an integrated mindset. We need to maintain flexibility across the various modes of thinking—including our autopilot, reflective thinking, and sensory salience modes. Such flexibility requires a well functioning prefrontal cortex. However, it should be obviously clear by now that the prefrontal cortex never does anything by itself. Remember—*it's the whole brain stupid*!

Get Thinking!

Coordinate	Work on integrating thoughts in new ways—fire and wire together!
Cognitive Control	Plan, organize, and adapt to changes—use your prefrontal cortex!
Useful Thinking	Start a project, take the initiative, react to the world around you.
Make it Fresh	Think about doing something different every day.
Did You Know?	Expand your knowledge through internet sources (*YouTube, Wiki*).

Epilogue

By 2030 there will be more individuals in the U. S. over 65 than under 15 years of age. To assure a healthy aging culture we all need to foster an active mental lifestyle and a sense of lifelong learning. It is rather simple: *Get Social!*, *Get Moving!*, *Get Artistic!*, *Get Responsive!*, and *Get Thinking!* I am not advocating a myth of ageless existence; we cannot and should not act like Peter Pan. However, we can develop daily activities that will keep our brains as healthy as possible.

Getting social is the most critical step. By engaging in the art of social conversation, you force yourself to move, create, respond, and think. For some people, social engagement is as easy as walking. For others, such as myself, reading, writing, or watching a good movie is preferable to parties and other social events. Regardless of your social inclinations, take the initiative to converse with family, friends, and even strangers. Schedule social occasions that cater to your interests. If you like to read, write, or watch movies, join a group that meets regularly to chat about such activities. It is to your advantage to get out in the world and interact with it. Your brain was built for the very purpose of social engagement.

What about our genes? The party line used to be that our genetic makeup is what it is, and we really cannot do anything about. Thus, our destiny is programmed, and we age and die according to our genetic blueprint. It is true that some are blessed with "good" genes that increase the chances of living to 100 years, whereas others have genes that increase the probability of having Alzheimer's disease. Yet how our genes are expressed depends significantly on our lifestyle now and how well we maintained ourselves throughout our lives. Although we all have our own specific genetic blueprint, how these genes are expressed can be determined by environmental factors. For example, a major aspect of gene expression is its control or regulation. Cells switch on and off gene expression, and this genetic switch can be influenced by environmental factors.

Another interesting feature is the way *telomeres* operate. Telomeres are repetitive sequences of DNA at the ends of each chromosome that protect the chromosome from deteriorating. These endpoints shorten with each replication, and thus as we age the ability of telomeres to protect our chromosomes weakens. This form of "cellular aging" offers a key to developing ways of protecting our DNA. If we can keep our telomeres in place, we may be able to forestall the aging process. Medical research is searching for drugs that focus on protecting telomeres. Interestingly, those who are physically active appear to have more intact telomeres than less active individuals.

Recently, gerontologists have studied successful agers. "Longevity genes" in centenarians appear to protect them from life-shortening diseases, such as cancer, diabetes, osteoporosis, and cardiovascular disease. The number of centenarians, however, is increasing, suggesting that lifestyle can play a significant role in living longer. Another research interest is *superagers*, elderly adults whose performance on memory tests is as good as adults in their 20s and 30s. These individuals have superior mental abilities and superior brains. MRI studies have shown that the cortical surface of superagers is more intact, particularly in brain regions related to thinking processes, such as the default mode network. In superagers, cortical regions that show typical age-related thinning were thick and comparable to the brains of young adults.

Around the world there are pockets of individuals who appear to age more successfully than normal. For example, inhabitants of Okinawa, a southern island in Japan, have one of the highest centenarian ratios in the world. Roughly 6.5 in 10,000 people live to be 100 years old, compared to the United States where 1.7 in 10,000 are centenarians. A major factor in the longevity of Okinawans is their diet, which consists largely of vegetables, fruits, and legumes, mostly soy (e.g., tofu). Moreover, they stress a low-calorie diet, which is expressed in their saying, *hara hachi-bu*, which translates to "eat until you are 80 percent full." This 80% rule should be a prime directive for all of us.

Michael Pollan, the noted food historian and health advocate, has made the following suggestion:

Eat food. Not too much. Mostly plants. He argues that there are simple guidelines for the prevention of Western ailments, such as high blood pressure, cardiovascular disease, diabetes, and obesity. In his book *Food Rules*, Pollan offers 64 basic rules to help maintain a healthy diet. The rules include, "If it came from a plant, eat it; if it was made in a plant, don't," "Serve a proper portion and don't go back for seconds," and "Eat all the junk food you want as long as you cook it yourself." He ends with Rule 64: "Break the rules once in a while."

A healthy diet is of course essential for both body and mind. The *Dietary Guidelines for Americans, 2015-2020* published by the Office of Disease Prevention and Health Promotion should be followed. Fill your plate with vegetables, fruits, whole grains (breads, cereals, crackers), low-fat dairy (low-fat yogurt, milk, cheese), and low-fat proteins (seafood, poultry, beans, and nuts). Avoid foods with added sugars (candies, cakes, cookies) or saturated fats (fried and processed foods, fatty meats and cheeses). Aim for 2000 calories per day, with each plate containing roughly 50% fruits and vegetables, 25% whole grains, and 25% low-fat protein.

Stuff happens. Injuries, accidents, diseases— events occur during our lives that cannot be controlled or anticipated. No matter how hard we work to maintain a healthy brain, there may be difficult or unavoidable stresses down the road. Nevertheless, it is critical to *stay positive*, as the adoption of a strong mental outlook is the most important factor in rebounding from any emotional or physical stress. Of course, it is easier said than done, but if you adhere to the *Get SMART!* program, you'll be on the road to recovery. It's not that you have be exceedingly optimistic or fall into to denying your stresses or predicaments. Indeed, as mentioned earlier, it is a good thing to be somewhat pessimistic, as it forces you to be conscientious and concerned. With a strong social network and healthy lifestyle, we can all work toward a positive mental attitude.

As a reminder of our steps toward a healthy brain, go back to the tables at the end of each chapter and consider implementing the tips on a daily basis. Encourage children and young adults to develop the program early on, as it is never too soon to begin preserving and fostering a healthy mental attitude. Most importantly, one is never too old to start, and the steps to get *social*, *moving*, *artistic*, *responsive*, and *thinking*, are simple yet effective. So *get going!* Keep active with a sense of lifelong learning and *Get SMART!*

References and Resources

Chapter 1: Get Started!

For up-to-date information on aging research and Alzheimer's disease, visit *National Institute on Aging.* Here's a worthy article: Forgetfulness: Knowing when to ask for help. https://www.nia.nih.gov/health/publication/forgetf ulness.

Albert, M. S., et al. (2011). The diagnosis of mild cognitive impairment due to Alzheimer's disease: Recommendations from the National Institute on Aging-Alzheimer's Association workgroups on diagnostic guidelines for Alzheimer's disease. *Alzheimer's & Dementia, 7,* 270–279.

Bakkour, A., Morris, J. C.,Wolk, D. A., Dickerson, B. C. (2013) The effects of aging and Alzheimer's disease on cerebral cortical anatomy: Specificity and differential relationships with cognition. *Neuroimage, 76,* 332–344.

Chun, M. (2016). Decoding the mind. *Future of Storytelling* website: https://futureofstorytelling.org/video/dr-marvin-chun-decoding-the-mind

D'Esposito, M. (2007). From cognitive to neural models of working memory. *Philosophical Transactions of the Royal Society London B Biological Science, 362*(1481), 761-772.

Danner, D. D., Snowdon, D. A., & Friesen, W. V. (2001). Positive emotions in early life and longevity: Findings from the Nun study. *Journal of Personality and Social Psychology, 80,* 804-813.

Diener, E. & Biswas-Diener, R. (2008). *Happiness: Unlocking the Mysteries of Psychological Wealth.* Wiley-Blackwell: New. York.

Gardner, H. E. (1983). *Frames of Mind. The Theory of Multiple Intelligences.* Basic Books. New York.

Gardner, H. E. (2006). *Multiple Intelligences: New Horizons in Theory and Practice.* Basic Books: New York.

Garrett, M.D. (2016). How mild is "Mild Cognitive Impairment"? *Psychology Today,* https://www.psychologytoday.com/blog/iage/2016 06/how-mild-is-mild-cognitive-impairment.

Gazzaley, A., & Rosen, L. D. (2016). *The Distracted Mind: Ancient Brains in a High-Tech World,* MIT Press: Cambridge, MA.

Huttenlocher, P. R. (1990). Morphometric study of human cerebral cortex development. *Neuropsychologia, 28,* 517-527.

Jeste, D. V., Depp, C. A., & Vahia, I. V. (2010). Successful cognitive and emotional aging. *World Psychiatry, 9,* 78-84.

Lipnicki, D. M., Crawford, J., Kochan, N. A., Trollor, J. M., Draper, B., and the Sydney Memory and Ageing Study Team. (2017). Risk factors for mild cognitive impairment, dementia and mortality: The Sydney Memory and Ageing Study. *JAMDA*, *18*, 388-395.

Low, L. K. & Cheng, H-J. (2006). Axon pruning: an essential step underlying the developmental plasticity of neuronal connections, *Phil. Trans. R. Soc. B, 361*, 1531–1544.

Mayo Clinic Staff (2016). Mild cognitive impairment (MCI). http://www.mayoclinic.org/diseases-conditions/mild-cognitive-impairment/home/ovc-20206082

Matthews, F. E. (2013). A two-decade comparison of prevalence of dementia in individuals aged 65 years and older from three geographical areas of England: results of the Cognitive Function and Ageing Study I and II. *The Lancet*, http://dx.doi.org/10.1016/S0140-6736(13)61570-6.

Park, D. C., & Festini, S. B. (2017). Theories of memory and aging: A Look at the past and a glimpse of the future. *The Journals of Gerontology Series B: Psychological Sciences and Social Sciences, 72*, 82-90.

Raz, N., Gunning-Dixon, F. M., Head, D., Dupuis, J. H., & Acker, J. D. (1998). Neuroanatomical correlates of cognitive aging: Evidence from structural magnetic resonance imaging. *Neuropsychology, 12*, 95-11.

Rowe, J. W., & Kahn, R. L. (1997). *Successful aging.* *The Gerontologist, 37,* 433–440.

Sapolsky, R. (2009). The uniqueness of humans. TED talk. https://www.ted.com/talks/robert_sapolsky_the_u niqueness_of_humans

Seligman, M. E.P. & Csikszentmihalyi, M.(2000). Positive psychology: An introduction. *American Psychologist, 55,* 5–14.

Shimamura, A. P. (2014). Remembering the past: Neural substrates underlying episodic encoding and retrieval. *Current Directions in Psychological Science, 23,* 257-263.

Shimamura, A. P., Berry, J. M., Mangels, J. A., Rusting, C. L., & Jurica, P. J. (1995). Memory and cognitive abilities in academic professors: Evidence for successful aging, *Psychological Science, 6,* 271-277.

Smith, K. (2013). Reading minds. *Nature, 502,* 427-430.

Snowdon, D. A. (2008). *Aging with Grace: What the Nun Study Teaches Us About Leading Longer, Healthier, and More Meaningful Lives,* Bantam Press: New York.

Chapter 2: Get Social!

AARP website on volunteering in your community: http://www.aarp.org/giving-back/ See also,

Experience Corp: http://www.aarp.org/experience-corps/

Agahi, N., & Parker, M. G. (2008). Leisure activities and mortality: Does gender matter? *Journal of Aging and Health*, 20, 855-871.

Anderson, N. D., Damianakis, T., Kröger, E., Wagner, L. M., Dawson, D. R., Binns, M. A., Bernstein, S., Caspi, E., Cook, S. L., & The BRAVO Team (2014). The benefits associated with volunteering among seniors: A critical review and recommendations for future research. *Psychological Bulletin. 140*, 1505-1533.

Barrett, L. F. (2017). *How Emotions are Made.* Macmillan Press: New York.

Bartz, J.A., Zaki, J., Bolger, N., & Ochsner, K N. (2011). Social effects of oxytocin in humans: Context and person matter. *Trends in Cognitive Science*, *15*, 301-309.

Beer, J. S., Shimamura, A. P. & Knight, R. T. (2004). Frontal lobe contributions to executive control of cognitive and social behavior. In M. S. Gazzaniga (Ed.), *The Cognitive Neurosciences*, 3rd Edition (pp. 1091-1104), MIT Press: Cambridge, MA.

Charles, S. T., & Carsensen, L. L. (2009). Social and emotional aging. *Annual Review of Psychology*, *62*, 383-409.

Chen, Y. & Feeley, T. H. (2013). Social support, social strain, loneliness, and well-being among older adults: An analysis of the Health and

Retirement Study. *Journal of Social Personal and Relationships,* 1-21.

Crooks, V. C., Lubben, J., Petitti, D. B., Little, D., & Chiu, V. (2008). Social network, cognitive function, and dementia: Incidence among elderly woman. *American Journal of Public Health, 98,* 1221-127.

De Vignemont, F., Singer, T. (2006). The empathic brain: how, when and why? *Trends in Cognitive Science, 10,* 435-441.

Fineberg, S. K. & Ross, D. A. (2017). Oxytocin and the social brain. *Biological Psychiatry, 81,* e19–e21.

Gallese, V., Keysers, C., & Rizzolatti, G. (2004). A unifying view of the basis of social cognition. *Trends in Cognitive Science, 8 ,* 396–403 .

Kemp, A. H. & Guastella, A. J. (2011). The role of oxytocin in human affect: A novel hypothesis. *Current Directions in Psychological Science, 20,* 222-231.

Mather, M. & Carstensen, L. L. (2005). Aging and motivated cognition: The positivity effect in attention and memory. *Trends in Cognitive Science, 9,* 496-502.

Oerlemans, W. G. M., Bakker, A. B., & Veenhoven, R. (2011). Finding the key to happy Aging: A day reconstruction study of happiness. Journal of Gerontology, B Psychological Science, 66B, 665-674.

Oh, H. J., Ozkaya, E., & LaRose, R. (2014). How does online social networking enhance life satisfaction? The relationships among online supportive interaction, affect, perceived social support, sense of community, and life satisfaction. *Computers in Human Behavior, 30,* 69-78.

Osher Lifelong Learning Institutes: http://www.osherfoundation.org/ index.php?olli_list

Pantell, M., Rehkopf, D., Jutte, D., Syme, S. L., Balmes, J., & Adler, N. (2013). Social isolation: A predictor of mortality comparable to traditional clinical risk factors. *American Journal of Public Health, 103,* 2056-2062.

Purcell, M. (2006). Making conversation: A skill, not an art. *Psych Central.*

http://psychcentral.com/lib/making-conversation-a-skill-not-an-art/000690

Rizzolatti, G. & Sinigaglia, C. (2016). The mirror mechanism: A basic principle of brain function. *Nature Reviews Neuroscience, 17,* 757-765.

Sapolsky, R. M. (2004). *Why Zebras Don't Get Ulcers.* Henry Holt and Co.: New York.

Saxe, R. (2006). Uniquely human social cognition. *Current Opinion in Neurobiology, 16,* 235-239.

Shen, H. (2015). The hard science of oxytocin. *Nature, 522,* 410-412.

Taylor, J. M. (2016). Mirror neurons after a quarter century: New light, new cracks. Harvard University Science in the News (SITN). http://sitn.hms.harvard.edu/flash/2016/mirror-neurons-quarter-century-new-light-new-cracks/

van Gelder, B. M., Tijhuis, M., Kalmijn, S., Giampaoli, S., Nissinen, A., Kromhout, D. (2006). Marital status and living situation during a 5-year period are associated with a subsequent 10-year cognitive decline in older men: the FINE Study. *Journals of Gerontology Series B: Psychological Sciences & Social Sciences, 61,* 213–219.

Chapter 3: Get Moving!

Alfini, A. J. Weiss, L.R., Leitner, B. P., Smith, T. J., Hagberg, J. M., Smith, J. C. (2016). Hippocampal and cerebral blood flow after exercise cessation in master athletes. *Frontiers in Aging Neuroscience, 8,* DOI: 10.3389/fnagi.2016.00184.

Basso, J.C., & Suzuki, W. A. (2017). The effects of acute exercise on mood, cognition, neurophysiology, and neurochemical pathways: A review. *Brain Plasticity, 2,* 127-152.

Bolandzadeh, N., Tam R., Handy, T. C., Nagamatsu, L. S., Hsu, C. L., Davis, J. C., Dao, E. , Beattie, B. L. , & Liu-Ambrose, T. (2015). Resistance training and white matter lesion progression in older women: Exploratory analysis of a 12-month randomized controlled trial. *Journal of the American Geriatric Society, 63*, 2052-2060.

Buchman, A. S., Boyle, P. A., Yu, L., Shah, R. C., Wilson, R. S., & Bennett, D. A. (2012), Total daily physical activity and the risk of AD and cognitive decline in older adults. *Neurology, 78*, 1323-1329.

Centers for Disease Control and Prevention (2015). How much physical activity do older adults need? http://www.cdc.gov/physicalactivity/everyone/guidelines/olderadults.html

Colcombe, S. J., Erickson, K. I., Scalf, P. E., Kim, J. S., Prakash, R., McAuley, E., & Kramer, A. F. (2006). Aerobic exercise training reduces brain tissue loss in aging humans. *Journals of Gerontology Series A: Biological Sciences and Medical Sciences, 61*(11), 176–180.

Csikszentmihaly, M. (1990). *Flow: The Psychology of Optimal Experience*. Harper & Row: New York.

Dougherty, R., Schultz, S. A, Kirby, T. K., Boots, E. A., Oh, J. M., et al. (2017). Moderate physical activity is associated with cerebral glucose metabolism in adults at risk for Alzheimer's Disease. *Journal of Alzheimer's Disease, 58*, 1089-1097.

Gothe, N. P., Kramer, A. F., & McAuley, E. (2017). Hatha Yoga practice improves attention and processing speed in older adults: Results from an 8-week randomized control trial. *The Journal of*

Alternative and Complementary Medicine, 23, 35-40.

Grierson, B. (2010). The incredible flying nonagenarian. *New York Times Magazine* (November 25, 2010). http://www.nytimes.com/2010/11/28/magazine/28 athletes-t.html

Hall, K.G., Domingues, D.A., & Cavazos, R. (1994). Contextual interference effects with skilled baseball players. *Perceptual and Motor Skills, 78,* 835-841.

Hamer, M., Lovoie, K. L., & Bacon, S. L. (2014). Taking up physical activity in later life and healthy ageing: the English longitudinal study of ageing. *British Journal of Sports Medicine, 48,* 239-243.

Kempermann, G., Wiskott, L., & Gage, F. H. (2004). Functional significance of adult neurogenesis. *Current Opinion in Neurobiology, 14,* 186–191.

Nagamatsu, L. S., Chan, A., Davis, J. C., et al. (2013). Physical activity improves verbal and spatial memory in older adults with probable mild cognitive impairment: a 6-month randomized controlled trial. *Journal of Aging Research, 2013,* 1-10.

Nagamatsu, L. S., Flicker, L., Kramer, A. F., Voss, M. W., Erickson, K. I., Hsu, C. L., & Liu-Ambrose, T. (2014). Exercise is medicine, for the body and the brain. *British Journal of Sports Medicine. 48,* 943-944.

Onushko, T., Kim, C., & Christou, E. A. (2014). Reducing task difficulty during practice improves motor learning in older adults. *Experimental Gerontology, 57,* 168-174.

Pereira, A. C., Huddleston, D. E., Brickman, A. M., Sosunov, A. A., Hen, R., et. Al. (2007). An *in vivo* correlate of exercise-induced neurogenesis in the adult dentate gyrus. *Proceedings of the National Academy of Sciences, 104,* 5638-5643.

Pollock, M. L., Franklin, B. A., Balady, G. J., Chaitman, B. L., Fleg, J. L. et al. (2000). Resistance exercise in individuals with and without cardiovascular disease. *Circulation, 101,* 828-833.

Pollock, R. D., Carter, S., Velloso, C. P., Duggal, N. A., Lord, J. M., Lazarus, N. R., & Harridge, S. D. R. (2015). An investigation into the relationship between age and physiological function in highly active older adults. *Journal of Physiology, 593,* 657–680.

Reid, K. J., Baron, K. G., Lu, B., Naylor, E., Wolfe, L., Zee, P. C. (2010). Aerobic exercise improves self-reported sleep and quality of life in older adults with insomnia. *Sleep Medicine, 11,* 934-940.

Reynolds, G. (2017). The best exercise for aging muscles. *The New York Times* (March 23).

https://www.nytimes.com/2017/03/23/well/move/the-best-exercise-for-aging-muscles.html?_r=0

Sacred Journeys:
http://www.pbs.org/wgbh/sacredjourneys/content/home/

Schmidt-Kassow,M., Deusser, M., Thiel, C., Otterbein, S., Montag, C., Reuter, M., Banzer, W., & Kaiser, J. (2013). Physical exercise during encoding improves vocabulary learning in young female adults: A neuroendocrinological study. *PLOS ONE, 8*, e64172.

Schuch, F. B., Vancampfort, D., Sui, X., Rosenbaum, S., Firth, J., Richards, J., Ward, P. B, & Stubbs, B. (2016). Are lower levels of cardiorespiratory fitness associated with incident depression? A systematic review of prospective cohort studies. *Preventive Medicine, 93*, 159-165.

Shors, T. J. (2014). The adult brain makes new neurons, and effortful learning keeps them alive. *Current Directions in Psychological Sciences, 23*, 311–318.

Sifferlin, A. (2016). Exercise keeps the brain young. *Time Magazine*, http://time.com/4619686/exercise-cognitive-decline/

Smith, J. C., Nielson K., Antuono P., Lyons, J-A., Hanson, R. J., Butts, A. M., Hantke, N. C., & Verber, M. D. (2013). Semantic memory functional MRI and cognitive function after exercise intervention in mild cognitive impairment. *Journal of Alzheimer's Disease, 37,* 197-215.

Suzuki,W. TED talk, youtube.com/watch?v=LdDnPYr6R0o

van Praag, H., Kempermann, G., & Gage, F. H. (1999). Running increases cell proliferation and neurogenesis in the adult mouse dentate gyrus. *Nature Neuroscience, 2,* 266–270.

Voss, M. W., Prakash, R. S., Erickson, K. I., Basak, C., Chaddock, L., et al. (2010). Plasticity of brain networks in a randomized intervention trial of exercise training in older adults. *Frontiers in Aging Neuroscience, 2,* 1-17.

Voss, M. W., Vivar, C., Kramer, A. F., & van Praag, H. (2013). Bridging animal and human models of exercise-induced brain plasticity. *Trends in Cognitive Science, 17,* 525–544.

Chapter 4: Get Artistic!

For information about the ARTZ program, see http://www.imstillhere.org/artz

Arden, R., Chavez, R. S., Grazioplene, R., & Jung, R. E. (2010). Neuroimaging creativity: A psychometric view. *Behavioural Brain Research, 25,* 143-156.

Bagan, B. (2017). Aging: What's art got to do with it? *Today's Geriatric Medicine,* http://www.todaysgeriatricmedicine.com/news/ex_082809_03.shtml

Blood, A. J. & Zatorre, R. J. (2011). Intensely pleasurable responses to music correlate with activity in brain regions implicated in reward and emotion. *Proceedings of the National Academy of Sciences, 98,* 11818–11823.

Brody, J. E. (2016). Using the arts to promote healthy aging. *The New York Times,* https://well.blogs.nytimes.com/2016/03/07/using-the-arts-to-promote-healthy-aging/?ref=health&_r=1

Chancellor, B., Duncan, A., & Chatterjee, A. (2014). Art therapy for Alzheimer's Disease and other dementias. *Journal of Alzheimer's Disease, 39,* 1-11.

Chrysikou, E. G., & Thompson-Schill, S. L. (2011). Dissociable brain states linked to common and creative object use. *Human Brain Mapping, 32,* 665-675.

Espinel, C. H. (1996). de Kooning's late colours and forms: Dementia, creativity, and the healing power of art. *Lancet, 347,* 1096-1098.

Fink, A., Benedek, M., Grabner, R. H., Staudt, B., Neubauer, A. C. (2007). Creativity meets neuroscience: Experimental tasks for the neuroscientific study of creative thinking. *Methods, 42,* 68-76.

Flatt, J. D., Liptak, A., Oakley, M. A., Gogan, J., Varner, T., Lingler, J. H. (2015). Subjective experiences of an art museum engagement activity for persons with early-stage Alzheimer's disease and their family caregivers. *American Journal of Alzheimer's Disease and Other Dementia, 30*, 380-389.

Keith Jarrett on listening while improvising. *National Public Radio* Interview, May 10, 2015. http://www.npr.org/2015/05/10/404975326/

Limb, C. J., & Braun, A. R. (2008). Neural substrates of spontaneous music performance: An fMRI study of jazz improvisation. *PLoS ONE, 3*, 2-9.

López-González, M. & Limb, C. J. (2012). Musical creativity and the brain. *Cerebrum*, February, 2012, http://dana.org/Cerebrum/Default.aspx?id=39472

Rentz, C. A. (2002). Memories in the making: Outcome-based evaluation of an art program for individuals with dementing illnesses. *American Journal of Alzheimer's Disease and Other Dementias, 17*, 175-181.

Rodman, S. (1957). *Conversations with Artists*. New York : Devin-Adair.

Salimpoor, V. N., Benovoy, M., Larcher, K., Dagher, A., & Zatorre R. J. (2011). Anatomically distinct dopamine release during anticipation and experience of peak emotion to music. *Nature Neuroscience, 14*, 258-264.

Shimamura, A. P. (2013). *Experiencing Art: In the Brain of the Beholder.* Oxford University Press: Oxford.

Simonton, D. K. (2012). Teaching creativity: Current findings, trends, and controversies in the psychology of creativity. *Teaching of Psychology, 39,* 217-222.

Sternberg, R. J. (2016). Creativity, intelligence, and culture. In V.P. Glăveanu (ed.), *Palgrave Handbook of Creativity and Culture Research, Palgrave Studies in Creativity and Culture* (pg. 77-99). New York: Cambridge University Press.

Verghese, J., Lipton, R. B., Katz, M. J., Hall, C. B., Derby, C. A., Kuslansky, G., Ambrose, A. F., Sliwinski, M., & Buschke, H. (2003). Leisure activities and the risk of dementia in the elderly. *The New England Journal of Medicine, 348,* 2508-2516.

Wai, J. (2014). Experts are born, then made: Combining prospective and retrospective longitudinal data shows that cognitive ability matters. *Intelligence, 45,* 74-80.

Chapter 5: Get Responsive!

Here are some websites that can help you find places to volunteer your services: Senir Corps (www.getinvolved.gov), United We Serve (www.serve.gov), VolunteerMatch (www.volunteermatch.org).

Popular free sites for blogging include *Blogger* (blogger.com), Tumblr (tumblr.com), and *WordPress* (wordpress.com).

Einstein, G.O., Mullet, H.G., & Harrison, T.L. (2012). The testing effect: Illustrating a fundamental concept and changing study strategies. *Teaching of Psychology, 39*, 190-193.

Friedman, H. S., & Martin, L. R. (2012). *The Longevity Project: Surprising Discoveries for Health and Long Life from the Landmark Eight-Decade Study*, Plume: New York.

Karpicke, J.D., & Blunt, J.R. (2011). Retrieval practice produces more learning than elaborative studying with concept mapping. *Science, 331*, 772-775.

Karpicke, J. D. (2016). A powerful way to improve learning and memory. Psychological Science Agenda (June Issue).

http://www.apa.org/science/about/psa/2016/06/learning-memory.aspx

Lang, F.R., Weiss, D., (2013). Forecasting life satisfaction across adulthood: Benefits of seeing a dark future? *Psychology and Aging, 28*, 249-261.

Lengenfelder, J., Chiaravalloti, N. D., DeLuca, J. (2007). The efficacy of the generation effect in improving new learning in persons with traumatic brain injury. *Rehab. Psychol.* 52, 290-296.

Oppenheimer, F. (1975). The Exploratorium and other ways of teaching physics. *Physics Today 28*, 9-13.

Park, D. C., Gutchess, A. H., Meade, M. L., & Stine-Morrow, E. A. L. (2007). Improving cognitive function in older adults: Nontraditional approaches. *Journal of Gerontology: Series B, 62B*, 45–52.

Putnam, A. L., Sungkhasettee, V. W., & Roediger, H. L. (2016). Optimizing learning in college: Tips From cognitive psychology. *Perspectives on Psychological Science, 11*, 652-660.

Riley, K. P., Snowdon, D. A., Desrosiers, M. F., & Markesbery, W. R. (2005). Early life linguistic ability, late life cognitive function, and neuropathology: Findings from the Nun Study. *Neurobiology of Aging, 26*, 341-347.

Roediger, H. L., & Butler, A. C. (2011). The critical role of retrieval practice in long-term retention. *Trends in Cognitive Science, 15*, 20-27.

Rosner, Z. A., Elman, J. A. & Shimamura, A. P. (2013). The generation effect: Activating broad neural circuits during memory encoding. *Cortex, 49*, 1901-1909.

Soderstrom, N. C., Kerr, T. K., & Bjork, R. A. (2016). The critical importance of retrieval— and spacing—for learning. *Psychological Science, 27*, 223-230.

Souliez, L., Pasquier, F., Lebert, F., Leconte, P., Petit, H. (1996). Generation effect in short term verbal and visuospatial memory: comparisons between dementia of the Alzheimer type and dementia of the frontal lobe type. *Cortex* 32, 347–356.

Chapter 6: Get Thinking!

A consensus on the brain training industry from the scientific community (October, 15, 2014). http://longevity3.stanford.edu/blog/2014/10/15/the -consensus-on-the-brain-training-industry-from-the-scientific-community-2/

Buckner, R. L. (2013). The brain's default network: origins and implications for the study of psychosis *Dialogues in Clinical Neuroscience, 15*, 351-358.

Cabeza R., Anderson, N. D. , Locantore, J. K. , McIntosh, A. R. (2002). Aging gracefully: Compensatory brain activity in high-performing older adults. *NeuroImage*, 17, 1394–1402.

Cavanagh, J. F. & Frank, M. J. (2014). Frontal theta as a mechanism for cognitive control. *Trends in Cognitive Science, 18*, 414-421.

Chan, M. Y., Haber, S., Drew, L. M., & Park, D. C. (2016). Training older adults to use tablet computers: Does it enhance cognitive function? *The Gerontologist, 56*, 475-484.

Cho, J. (2016). Six scientifically proven benefits Of mindfulness and meditation. Forbes (July 14). https://www.forbes.com/sites/jeenacho/2016/07/14 /10-scientifically-proven-benefits-of-mindfulness-and-meditation/#7ea4c64763ce

Doll, A., Holzel, B. K.,Bratec, S. M., Boucard, C. C., Xie,X., Wohlschlager,A. M., & Sorg, C. (2016). Mindful attention to breath regulates emotions via increased amygdala-prefrontal cortex circuitry. *NeuroImage*, *134*, 305–313.

F.T.C.'s Lumosity Penalty Doesn't End Brain Training Debate, *New York Times* (January 16, 2016). http://www.nytimes.com/2016/01/19/health/ftcs-lumosity-penalty-doesnt-end-brain-training-debate.html?_r=0

Goyal, M., Singh, S., Sibinga, E M. S., Gould, N. F., Rowland-Seymour, A., et al. (2014). Meditation programs for psychological stress and well-being: A systematic review and meta-analysis. *Journal of the American Medical Association: Internal Medicine*, *174*, 357-368.

Hulsheger, U. R., Lang, J. W. B., Depenbrock, F., Fehrmann, C., Zijlstra, F. R. H., & Alberts, H. J. E. M. (2014). The power of presence: The role of mindfulness at work for daily levels and change trajectories of psychological detachment and sleep quality. *Journal of Applied Psychology*, *99*, 1113-1128.

Knight, R.T. (1996) Contribution of human hippocampal region to novelty detection. *Nature*, *383*, 256-259. Kumaran, D., & Maguire, E. A. (2009). Novelty signals: A window into hippocampal information processing. *Trends in Cognitive Science, 13*, 47-54.

Krieger, L. (2016). Mindfulness workouts are the new way to work your body and brain. *Self* (Dec Issue), http://www.self.com/story/mindfulness-workouts-body-brain.

Lutz, A., Jha, A. P., Dunne, J. D., & Saron, C. D. (2015). Investigating the phenomenological matric of mindfulness-related practices from a neurocognitive perspective. *American Psychologist, 70*, 632-658.

Lutz, J., Bruhl, A. B., Scheerer, H.,Jancke, L., Herwig, U. (2016). Neural correlates of mindful self-awareness in mindfulness meditators and meditation-naïve subjects revisited. *Biological Psychology, 119*, 21-30.

Mishra, J., Anguera, J. A., Gazzaley, A. (2016). Video games for neurocognitive optimization. *Neuron, 90*, 214-218.

Park, D. C., Lodi-Smith, J., Drew, L., Haber, S., Hebrank, A., Bischof, G. N., & Aamodt, W. (2014). The impact of sustained engagement on cognitive function in older adults: The Synapse Project. *Psychological Science, 25*, 103-12.

Park, D. C., Reuter- Park D. C., Reuter-Lorenz, P. A. (2009). The adaptive brain: aging and neurocognitive scaffolding. *Annual Review of Psychology, 2*, 173–196.

141

Persson, N., Ghisletta, P., Dahle, C. L., Bender, A. R., Yang, Y., Yuan, P., Daugherty, A. M., & Raz,N. (2016). Regional brain shrinkage and change in cognitive performance over two years: The bidirectional influences of the brain and cognitive reserve factors. *Neuroimage, 126*, 15-26.

Rajah, M.N., D'Esposito, M. (2005). Region-specific changes in prefrontal function with age: a review of PET and fMRI studies on working and episodic memory. *Brain, 128*, 1964-1983.

Seeley, W. W., Menon, V., Schatzberg, A. F., Keller, J., Glover, G. H., Kenna, H. Reiss, A. L., & Greicius, M. D. (2007). Dissociable intrinsic connectivity networks for salience processing and executive control. *The Journal of Neuroscience, 27*, 2349-2356.

Simons, D.J., Boot, W. R., Charness, N., Gathercole, S. E., Chabris, C. F., Hambrick, D. Z., & Stine-Morrow, E. A. L. (2016). Do "brain-training" programs work? *Psychological Science in the Public Interest, 17*, 103-186.

Shimamura, A. P. (2008). A neurocognitive approach to metacognitive monitoring and control. In J. Dunlosky & R. A. Bjork (Eds), *Handbook of Metamemory and Memory* (pp. 373-390). Psychology Press: New York.

Shors, T. J., Olson, R. L., Bates, M. E., Selby, E. A., & Alderman, B. L. (2014). Mental and physical (MAP) training: A neurogenesis-inspired intervention that enhances health in humans. *Neurobiology of Learning and Memory, 115*, 3-9.

Simons, D. J., Boot, W. R., Charness, N., Gathercole, S. E., Chabris, C. F., Hambrick, D. Z., Stine-Morrow, E. A. L. (2016). Do "brain-training" programs work? *Psychological Science in the Public Interest, 17*, 103-186.

Smart, C. M., Segalowitz, S. J., Mulligan, B. P., Koudys, J., & Gawryluk, J. R. (2016). Mindfulness training for older adults with subjective cognitive decline: Results from a pilot randomized controlled trial. *Journal of Alzheimer's Disease. 52*, 757-74.

Stern, Y. (2000). What is cognitive reserve? Theory and research application of the reserve concept. *Journal of the International Neuropsychological Society, 8*, 448–460.

Epilogue

A video of *Get SMART!* was presented at the end of my talk to the UC Berkeley Retirement Center, *Human Memory, Aging, and the Brain or Where Did I Put Those Keys?* www.youtube.com/watch?v=eKcxrB_epTU&list= PLY2PHbIE-XUyrnoFPK__qHJt3BKz_ U6tk&index=1

Cook, A. H., Sridhar,J., Ohm, D., et al. (2017). Rates of cortical atrophy in adults 80 years and older with superior vs average episodic memory.

Journal of the American Medical Association, 317, 1373-1375.

Gefen, T, Shaw, E., Whitney, K., Martersteck, A., Stratton, J., Rademaker, A., Weintraub, S., Mesulam, M. M., Rogalski, E (2014) Longitudinal neuropsychological performance of cognitive SuperAgers. *Journal of American Geriatric Society, 62*, 1598 –1600.

Mansfield, S. (2015). Food for thought: A traditional Okinawan diet may help prolong life. *The Japan Times* (Dec 12).

http://www.japantimes.co.jp/life/2015/12/12/lifestyle/ food-thought-traditional-okinawan-diet-may-help-prolong-life/#.WUbAQzPMxbg

Office of Disease Prevention and Health Promotion (2015). *Dietary Guidelines for Americans, 2015-2020.*

https://health.gov/dietaryguidelines/2015/guidelin es/

Pollan, M. (2009) *Food Rules: An Eater's Manual.* Penguin Books: New York.

Shammas, M. A. (2011). Telomeres, lifestyle, cancer, and aging. *Current Opinions in Clinical Nutrition Metabolic Care, 14, 28-34.*

Sun, F. W., Stepanovic, M. R., Andreano, J., Barrett, L. F., Touroutoglou, A., & Dickerson, B. C. (2016). Youthful brains in older adults: Preserved neuroanatomy in the default mode and salience networks contributes to youthful memory in superaging. *Journal of Neuroscience, 36,* 9659-9668.

Toder, F. (2016). Positive aging movement takes off. *Huffington Post* (May 18), http://www.huffingtonpost.com/francine-toder-phd/positive-aging-movement-t_b_7295650.html

Tucker, L. A. (2017). Physical activity and telomere length in U.S. men and women: An NHANES investigation, *Preventive Medicine, 100,* 145-151.

Made in the USA
Middletown, DE
14 July 2017